Fumbling

Fumbling

A Pilgrimage Tale of Love, Grief, and Spiritual Renewal on the Camino de Santiago

Kerry Egan

Doubleday

New York London Toronto Sydney Auckland

PUBLISHED BY DOUBLEDAY
a division of Random House, Inc.

DOUBLEDAY and the portrayal of an anchor with a dolphin are registered trademarks of Random House, Inc.

Book design by Donna Sinisgalli

Library of Congress Cataloging-in-Publication Data

Egan, Kerry.
Fumbling : a pilgrimage tale of love, grief, and spiritual renewal on the camino de Santiago / Kerry Egan.
p. cm.
ISBN 0-385-50765-8 (alk. paper)
1. Christian pilgrims and pilgrimages—Spain—Santiago de Compostela.
2. Egan, Kerry—Travel—Spain—Santiago de Compostela. 3. Santiago de Compostela (Spain)—Description and travel. I. Title.

BX2321.S3E43 2004
263'.042611-dc22 2004045484

PRINTED IN THE UNITED STATES OF AMERICA

October 2004

First Edition

1 3 5 7 9 10 8 6 4 2

For Alex Ruskell,

and in memory of my father

Be for them, Lord, a defence in emergency, a harbour in shipwreck, a refuge in the journey, shade in the heat, light in the darkness, a staff on the slippery slope, joy amidst suffering, consolation in sadness, safety in adversity, caution in prosperity, so that these your servants, under your leadership, may arrive where they are boldly going, and may return unharmed, and the church which laments their absence may experience the joy of their safe and prosperous return . . .

—*From a liturgy for those setting off on pilgrimage, The Missal of Vich,* A.D. *1038*

Them's got ears, let them hear
Them's got eyes, let them see . . .

—*Woody Guthrie*

PART 1

Fumbling

1.

Along the walls of the church in Navar, there are oil paintings of saints instead of windows. Yellow bones in tarnished reliquaries, faded plastic flowers, and plaster statues crowd tables pressed up against the stone walls. Since the only light in the dense darkness comes from the candles reflecting off the swirling columns of the gold altarpiece that stretches to the ceiling, objects emerged from the murk only as I passed by them, disappearing again as I stepped away. The cool dampness turned the layer of dust on my skin into a paste.

I knelt in the back of the church, my forehead on the top lip of the smooth, varnished pew in front of me. The wood was hard against my forehead, but not rough or uncomfortable, and after a while it felt as though my skin had begun to wrap itself around the pew, and that the wood had begun to mold to my head. I hadn't noticed that the evening's pilgrim's Mass had ended. I'd been crying for a long time, and I was startled and confused when I first sensed a gentle hovering presence all around me. Then I heard rubber soles squeaking against the stone floor.

Five or six old Spanish women in black cotton housedresses and thick glasses, with wrinkled necks and lips fallen in on themselves, crept down the aisles and slid across the pews toward me. Their backs hunched over in the light cardigan sweaters they wore to take the chill off in the still church air. They held rosary beads and pocketbooks close to their bodies. Very slowly and wordlessly moving closer, the women were encircling where I sat, until they stopped, scattered in the pews twelve or so feet from me.

The women said nothing, never got too close. They didn't make any motions to comfort or interrupt me, and though they could not know why I was crying, they did not ask. They did not know my father died one year ago on that day, or that all day I had steadfastly refused to think about him. Instead, I spent the afternoon as I walked along the Camino de Santiago, an old pilgrimage route in northern Spain, seething at the sun that burned the backs of my legs no matter how much sunscreen I put on, the prickly heat that erupted all over my belly no matter how long I soaked in cold water, the landscape with nothing tall enough to create shadows long enough to walk under, and the sky without a single cloud in it. There was nothing I could do to make it rain, to create shade, to cool the sun. I could not move the Camino under the trees in the distance. I could not move the towns closer together. I could not tell my father the things I wanted him to know, and I could not apologize for the many things I said to a sad, sick man.

A year had gone by and I could not change any of it, even if I worked very hard, was kind to strangers, begged God. I tried all those things, but I still quivered with regret all the time. I didn't know why I'd ever thought that walking four hundred miles to look at the supposed remains of Saint James—believed to have been washed ashore in a stone boat on the west coast of Spain after his death in Jerusalem—was a good idea. I didn't think I believed in God, let alone all these trappings of the religion I grew up with, for I saw little evidence to prove that God exists.

The women in the church did not know any of this. They just sat, breathing deep and long sighs, murmuring as they said their prayers around me, clicking their rosary beads as they settled their heavy bodies into the pews. Slow breath in, and a pause. A steady exhale. A rest. And then it began again. Their steady breathing steadied my own, and with ragged gulps I stopped crying. Just as slowly and silently as they came, they made their way away from me and out the door.

I sat in the pew for a few more minutes and watched the gold light at the front of the church pulsate through the remnants of tears in my eyes. Alex walked over, slid down the pew to sit next to me and said, "There's a wax effigy of a saint in a glass coffin in the back of the church . . ." His voice trailed up in a hopeful question while his eyes, which change from blue to green depending on the light, searched my face from behind his glasses. Everyone comforts in his own way; Alex's way usually involves the absurd.

We walked back to the pale effigy with disheveled black wig and faded clothing. I smiled for him. Then we pushed the door of the church open and stepped into the sunlight, still blinding even in the evening, reflecting off the paving stones of the square.

With the dark cloth of their dresses contrasted against the bleached yellow-gold of the buildings and street, the old ladies stood in a circle talking. The circle opened as I walked past, and the women, with jaws firmly set, looked at me.

One of them nodded very slowly. It was not a nod of acknowledgment, but a continuous nod, one of agreement.

I often wonder now what the woman was saying yes to, what that nod meant. I didn't wonder then. Yes meant yes, and for that moment, it made sense.

2.

Though I was in a strange world on the Camino, with a foreign language and foreign food, odd experiences and odd people, the strangeness of it didn't bother me too much. In some ways I had been a stranger to myself for many months.

I was a student at Harvard Divinity School, but didn't really understand or care about anything I read or heard in class. I slept sixteen hours every night and lived on Cheerios, pizza, and ice cream. Whole days went by during which I did nothing but sit on the couch. I didn't watch TV or read or nap. I just sat. I wasn't sad or lonely or angry or happy. I was doing surprisingly well after my father died, I thought. I didn't feel a thing.

He died in June after three months in the hospital for sepsis, but he had been very sick before that. He had been in the hospital on six different machines and twenty different tubes before, and I had thought he was going to die then, had steeled myself, but he didn't die. The strangest part of that spring was that this hospitalization felt exactly the same to me as all his others, only the end result was so different. I was well rehearsed in these long hospitalizations, had over twenty years of learning how to make the lump of anxiety in my stomach sit quietly, of splitting my practical and emotional lives between the private and almost secretive world of sickness and the outer world of school and friends and jobs. But I didn't know how to respond when he actually did die.

And that I was relieved, and that I couldn't feel sad because I did not miss him because I was angry at him, so angry at what he had become and what I thought he had done to everyone in my family—this left me without knowing what to think of myself. It was easy not to love while he was still alive, but what did it mean to not love when he was dead? To be glad that my mother's house no longer smelled like illness? To be relieved? It's not that I didn't know what to think. It's that I could barely stand what I thought.

The more compassion and kindness people shared, the more I began to avoid people, all people, spending more and more time on my couch, the weight of shame pinning me down. Even this, though, didn't register as a feeling. It was physical—a heaviness in the diaphragm and bowels, relieved only by the thought that I didn't have to take the bus down to Long Island that weekend, that I didn't have to go between worlds, between the world of books and blooming crab apple trees and the world of beeping machines and foul smells and the heavy mix of fear and longing that it end. The two worlds didn't seem to understand each other at all and I was tired of splitting myself in two.

A FRIEND FROM divinity school mentioned one day that she wanted to walk the Camino de Santiago. I'd never heard of it, and I'd read only a single book about pilgrimage that fall, but I decided that walking to Santiago was exactly what I should do. I had no idea why I wanted to go on a pilgrimage to a Christian holy place, since I didn't believe in a God I would want to spend energy and money trying to get to know, especially after having just witnessed what I considered his creation gone wrong. Of course, this was assuming God had even created any of this, for he didn't seem to have much power or desire to intervene. Nevertheless, I bought a guidebook on the Internet and explained my incoherent and ill-formed plan to Alex.

Alex and I began dating in our junior and sophomore years of college. He went to law school immediately after graduating because he thought it was expected, and because he believed it would make his parents happy. This trait of his, the desire to make others happy even at the expense of his own happiness, means that he often takes on burdens that shouldn't belong to him. He didn't like being an attorney, finding the confrontational aspects of it exhausting and the wool suits entirely too constricting and itchy. He moved to Somerville when I started divinity school, and within a few months Alex was making the biweekly bus trips with me.

He was sitting on the floor playing a video game, rocking and careening back and forth as his buxom female character fought off attack dogs and bandits. His broad swimmer's shoulders were hunched over the game controller.

"Spain, huh? That sounds cool. I like sangria." He paused to have his character pull out a bazooka. "And naps. They take siesta every day. I want to go, too."

"This is not going to be a vacation. This is a pilgrimage."

"Yeah, that sounds good. I like religious stuff. All those weird relics. Jawbones and kneecaps. Oh, shit." His character fell into a lake of fire.

"I really mean it, Alex. This isn't going to be like Prague, where you can just drink absinthe and go to pornographic puppet shows. We can't just stop in the middle and go to the Costa del Sol and get drunk every night. I am going to do this." My voice got louder as I spoke, almost shouting.

Alex turned around to face me. He furrowed his thick eyebrows, and light brown hair from his deep widow's peak flopped across his forehead. He spoke quietly. "And I want to help you. I know you're serious, and I want to go with you. I don't want you to be all alone. I'd worry about you." His crooked teeth broke into a small smile.

"What about your job?"

"Well, I know I definitely don't want to be a lawyer the rest of my life. Maybe I'll figure out what to do as a pilgrim. I know you don't believe me, but I really want to do this. I think it sounds great. I want to be a pilgrim. And I'd miss you and never sleep if you went alone."

"Well, if we go together, I'm in charge. I'm in charge of the pilgrimage."

"I'll be your Sancho Panza," he said mildly. He turned back around and started a new game.

THAT SPRING I carried my guidebook everywhere like a security blanket. I fell into step one day with a professor on his way to class, and showed him the book. "Are you going as a pilgrim or as an anthropologist?" he asked.

"A pilgrim," I said immediately. I was surprised at my answer though, because to be a pilgrim meant I believed in something, or at least hoped in something. I didn't know that about myself just then, along with a lot of other things I didn't know. The more I sat on the couch trying not to think or feel, the more disconnected from reality I became. My mind began to play weird tricks on me, and there were times when I sat there and could not quite figure out who I was or if I had any connection to the person I thought I had been. If I sat long enough, I began to doubt that I could actually know what was real at all. Those feelings of utter disconnection from yourself and the rest of the world, while scary, aren't uncommon in the first weeks or months of grieving, but at the time I didn't know that. I thought I was going crazy. And so the fact that I had enough hope to fly across the ocean and walk across a country to an ancient holy site I didn't believe in was a happy surprise, for hope is the belief that things can change. I wanted things to change.

Pilgrimage's emotional center is hope. One journeys perhaps out of devotion, or a longing for adventure, or, in my case, a confused and even desperate searching, but at the emotional heart of all those things is the idea that things can change for the better if one is willing to go somewhere else, a place where other people have gone with great hope, too, and been changed. But while I knew that I thought of myself as a pilgrim, journeying somewhere in search of something, I couldn't tell you what that something was.

When we left for Spain, all I knew about the Camino was the information from one guidebook describing its landmarks and history, another guide describing the pilgrim hostels and dining options in each town, and a pretty good understanding of the predominant theory on pilgrimage. I didn't talk to anyone who had actually done the Camino, nor had I even thought to read any of the many first-person accounts. I didn't know what to expect, and I suppose I actually expected both very little and a life-altering experience at the same time.

Two years through Harvard Divinity School and less than one year after my first and only significant personal loss, I frantically typed my last term paper three hours before our plane left.

"Just write a conclusion," Alex shouted from the bedroom as he shoved a random assortment of clothing into my bag for me. "It doesn't have to be good, it just has to pass."

I ran down the hill toward school in the sweet late-May air, past the flowering trees and under yellow-green leaves that had just opened in the blissfully long New England spring, shoved the paper under the professor's door, turned around, and ran back up the hill. Sweating and heaving, I got into the cab Alex had waiting at the curb. And without realizing it, I was a pilgrim.

3.

The barking came first, fast and sharp like a jackhammer. A black dog burst out of a dust cloud to our right, yellow fangs bared and lips crinkled back to his eyes; thick, ropy muscles straining in his chest and legs.

"Jesus!" Alex yelled. Burning sweat erupted in my armpits. To the left, a steep, weed-choked bank led to a river, to the right a rundown shack sat in the middle of hard-packed dirt, and ahead and behind us was just the wide-open road. There was nowhere to run to escape the dog. He roared closer, not stopping, not slowing, with his jaw hinged open. I turned toward the water, ready to dive in, when—

Thwunk! The dog's feet slid out and forward from under his body, then shot up to the sky. He landed on his back and grunted, his legs still running at full speed in the air. His collar was attached to a heavy chain that had stopped him three feet away from us.

A round woman with a purple kerchief on her head and checkerboard teeth in her wide smile emerged from the house and trotted toward us, giggling. "He scared you, didn't he? You were scared, right? Ha ha ha ha!"

I could barely stand. Alex was still standing with his feet planted apart, legs bent at the knee, ready to kick the dog in the face.

The dog scrambled up and shook the dust off, then looked around as though he were trying to see if anyone noticed. Alex stared him down. He slowly walked back to his steel doghouse, head hanging low, apparently resigned to a life of frustration.

"I keep him for thieves, to keep them away at night. He doesn't know the difference between thieves and pilgrims, so I know every time a pilgrim is coming. You're not the only ones he's scared!" She folded her hands on her belly, and smiled at us as if she had just told an exceptionally good joke.

My heart was still beating in my ears and I wasn't quite sure what to think. I definitely didn't get the joke.

"Come on." She waved to us to follow her and walked to the corrugated-steel hut just a few feet off the Camino and a few yards beyond her dog's matching house. A wide awning stretched out from the low tin roof, held up by wooden poles on either end. Under the awning, cans of soda and beer were neatly lined up on the edge of a counter and a large logbook lay open next to them. Rows of similar ledger books stood on shelves against the wall. Her house faced the weed-choked river we had been walking along, down in a little valley the water had carved. Some abandoned sheds, trash, and scrambling brush surrounded the building, but no other houses were around it. Just ahead and on the other side of the river, the castlelike white city of Logroño rose above our heads, separated from us by the water and a hill and a stone wall.

She pushed the book toward us and leaned forward. "You must sign. Here, sign right here." She pointed to a clear place in the ledger and handed us a pen.

On the wide, unlined paper messages were written in a dozen languages, in dozens of handwritings, some extravagantly taking up a whole page, some cramped into a corner, some written in the spaces left around the edges of other pilgrims' writing, as though trying to wind themselves around the other words for support or camouflage. Sketches and cartoons that pilgrims had drawn of themselves and their surroundings decorated a few of the messages. No one got by this woman or her dog without signing. The left-hand page and all the pages below it were crinkled and pockmarked with dried sweat and the pressure of people signing. The paper bubbled up as each page pushed against the pages above it, as though reaching up to the sky. The pages to the right, the untouched pages where no one had yet to sign a name, were clear, flat, quiet.

I wrote a short message and signed my name neatly, carefully, and in a straight line. I handed the pen to Alex, who wrote no message, instead signing his name quickly under mine in a loping and jagged hand. Then he drew the dog.

The woman carefully traced over our names with her finger, following the curves and slashes etched into the paper by the tip of the pen. She pointed to Alex's drawing and grinned. "That's good. You drew his teeth very well."

After a moment of staring at our names, she looked up and smiled. "Are you feeling better? Not so nervous? Would you like something to drink?" She nodded to the lined-up cans. I asked for a Lemon Kas, and Alex, though it was not yet ten o'clock in the morning, ordered a beer. I sipped the icy cold soda she pulled from a cooler, but Alex downed his beer in one long gulp. It was the only sign he gave that his nerves were frazzled by the dog.

She continued while we drank, "All the pilgrims who pass by here sign my books. For years and years, every single pilgrim." She pointed to the neat rows of books on the sagging shelves behind her. "All those books are filled with signatures, on every page. They know my work so well that they gave me my own *cello*. Give me your *credenciales* and I will stamp them."

We pulled out our *credenciales,* the pilgrims' "passports" that all walkers and bicyclists on the Camino carry, small thrice-folded cards stamped and dated in each town you go through that prove you are a pilgrim. The card allows a pilgrim to stay in the *refugios* and *albergues,* hostels that are run by churches and municipalities to provide cheap lodging for pilgrims. The *credenciale* is also presented to the Pilgrims' Office at the cathedral of Santiago, to prove pilgrimhood and earn a *Compostela,* the certificate given by the cathedral officially signifying completion of the pilgrimage. Basically, the *credenciale* confirmed your existence as a pilgrim—it was proof of your being at that point, at a place and time when all the things that usually identify who and what you are in this world cease to be relevant.

The woman's *cello,* or stamp, was a drawing of herself, and in purple ink she made her mark on our pilgrim's passports. She was Felicia, a "Friend of the Camino."

A few weeks later we learned from a hostel-keeper that Felicia is one of the best known of the many people who live along the Camino and dedicate their lives to it and to the pilgrims. He also told us that Felicia cannot read.

She never asked us what we wrote. The thank-yous, the jokes, the stories, and the poems dedicated to her are not the reward for her work, but rather the work itself. Having each and every pilgrim, for decades, sign his or her name—names never to be known by the gatherer—was her work; her calling, perhaps. In writing down my name, the tangible proof that I once passed this way, it was as though I had somehow signed myself into a new existence, as though Felicia were the gatekeeper of existence, of life itself, as though her dog were some sort of modern-day Cerberus and she Hades.

If I did not know who or what or how I was that summer, at least I knew that I did still exist. I could see the proof, and so could she, in my name in that book.

4.

Hope may be what keeps a pilgrim walking, but the idea underlying all pilgrimage is that some places are especially holy or sacred. Santiago de Compostela is believed to be one of those holy places. In the center of the cathedral, under the altar, is a silver casket said to contain the remains of Saint James. It is to these remains that a pilgrim journeys, to venerate the saint and ask him to intercede on one's behalf with God, and perhaps simply to live for a little while, from a few hours to a few weeks, in a place where the divide between God and humanity is narrower.

Legend says that Saint James preached on the Iberian peninsula in the years after Jesus' death and resurrection. He returned to Jerusalem where he was beheaded by Herod. His body was put into a stone boat and pushed into the Mediterranean, and landed back on the Spanish peninsula, in what is now the little town of Padrón. It was secretly retrieved and buried a few miles inland in Compostela, and then promptly forgotten. Several centuries later, the remains were miraculously found. Some say a hermit saw a mysterious light shining out from the burial place, and, drawn to it, stumbled across the tomb. Some say it was Charlamagne who found the remains in the midst of a military campaign to win the peninsula back from the Moors, a sign from God that Spain was meant to be Christian. A trickle at first, and then a flood of pilgrims journeyed to the northwestern, wet, and mountainous area of what became Spain, a place that was once believed to be the end of the world—the farthest western piece of land before the sea dropped off into the unknown. Pilgrims journeyed to pay homage to those remains that made their own miraculous journey.

Galicia, the region where Santiago is found, is still remote today. There are places along the Camino—where farmers till their fields with teams of oxen, or where ancient standing crosses carved with Romanesque images mark the way—where one could begin to believe she was not only walking across space, but across time as well.

WALKING TO THE remains of a saint is an old thing to do. The pilgrimage to Compostela had started by the ninth century, and by the thirteenth century, some scholars estimate half a million people walked to Santiago each year. Saint Francis walked the Camino in the thirteenth century, Queen Isabella and King Ferdinand in the fifteenth, and Shirley MacLaine the same year as Alex and I. Medieval towns thrived on the commerce of pilgrims, laying the groundwork for all sorts of aspects of modern life we take for granted, like hotels, hospitals, restaurants, souvenirs, and guidebooks.

There are actually many caminos de Santiago; all roads that lead to Compostela are pilgrimage roads if pilgrims take them. The route Alex and I walked is what most people mean when they refer to the Camino today; it is the Route Frances, where four main paths from four cities in France converge in Saint Jean Pied de Port, the point where the roads from northern Europe once met to cross the Pyrenees. At Puente la Reina, this road merges with the one coming from the south and east, which led pilgrims into Spain through Col de Somport. There were, through the centuries, other routes commonly traveled—a sea route from the British Isles, for example, and roads heading north from Portugal and southern Spain. But the most heavily traveled then and now is the Route Frances.

Today, the route walked—the Camino—has become as synonymous with the pilgrimage as the destination itself. The journey is as important to the pilgrimage as the holy place one journeys to, and for some pilgrims we met, much more so. It is as if the holiness of Santiago de Compostela has stretched out across a thin and winding strip of northern Spain, and the holy is encountered as readily on the road as in the cathedral.

From the little town of Saint Jean, the Camino crosses the Pyrenees and drops into the lush valleys of Navarra, the Basque country of Spain. It then heads west almost to the Atlantic. In between it passes through dozens of tiny villages, a few big cities, and many towns; across vineyards, wheat fields, and pastures; through forests and olive tree orchards, and over mountains.

PEOPLE HAVE BEEN journeying to sacred places for many thousands of years and pilgrimage as a recognizable form is found in all of the major world religions today, in varying guises and with varying levels of importance. Victor and Edith Turner, anthropologists whose ideas and theories about pilgrimage have deeply shaped the way scholars approach the phenomenon, suggest that the pilgrimage experience is one of liminality, a time in which a person is separate and apart from everyday life and expectations, apart from the normal patterns and strictures of society. A pilgrim is in an in-between space for a little while, a time both of great transition and great potential. In this place you can learn and experience things that it would not be possible to learn while not on pilgrimage. A pilgrim experiences *communitas,* the elimination of differences between people of different ages, classes, and nationalities. Barriers between people are thrown aside as a great feeling of unity and connectedness brings people together in a way that seems impossible within the regular structures of society. This *communitas* is a force that can transform society. On pilgrimage, the place is holy, but the journey itself—the time as a pilgrim—is transformative, cleansing, and purifying.

Pilgrims, at least for the time they are pilgrims, are different from other people, and pilgrimage sites are different from other places. Sometimes they have been recognized as sacred for a long, long time, through many different religions and peoples and cultures, as though the sacredness of the place is an integral characteristic of the geography, just as the soil might be dark loam or red clay, or the climate dry or wet. For example, some wells in Ireland have been sacred since before Patrick brought Christianity to Ireland; wells once sacred to the pre-Christian goddess Brighid are now sacred to the Virgin Mary. The understanding of why these places are sacred or to whom has changed as the religious beliefs and understanding of the people has changed, but the unique nature of the place remains as one set apart, different.

THE CAMINO IS made up of both the land—the physical surroundings and the physical work of getting through that land—and the people one meets, both fellow pilgrims and those who live along the route. The very act of pilgrimage—the jump from an idea to the action of walking hundreds of miles in a place where one is a complete stranger—is possible because of people like Felicia.

Is what makes the place sacred in the land itself, in the air, in the water, present since the earth was formed? Or is it all those prayers, millions of prayers, soaking into the dirt, into the rivers, into the plants, into the people who live along the way?

5.

"We're waiting for the shopkeeper," Ines said from the bench in front of the store. "She went to get the key to the church. We were told not to miss it."

Alex wanted a Coke and I wanted an ice cream, and since this was the only shop in the only town for the next few kilometers, we decided to wait.

Ines, an Australian woman with curly brown hair turning gray and round cheeks that broke out into a smile every few seconds, scooted down the bench, as her two traveling companions, a ranching couple in their seventies, slid in the other direction to make room for us in the middle. We had met them the day before in Estella when Ines gleefully pointed out the meat vending machine in the *refugio*. Shrink-wrapped portions of raw bacon, sausages, jerky, cutlets, and just about any red meat product you could think of, tumbled forward and down to a trapdoor at the bottom of the machine, just as gracefully as any candy bar.

The ranching couple didn't just sit on the bench but rested into it, their backs sinking into the stone wall they leaned against. The man's thin, sinewy legs and arms, leathered brown by the sun, and his chiseled face behind a white and slightly ragged beard barely moved, but his washed-out blue eyes seemed never to stop, gazing intensely at everything they rested on before quickly moving on. The woman's fluffy white hair moved softly with every current and breeze and she laughed quietly at almost everything her husband or Ines said. The three of them walked together. They didn't go far—just five or six kilometers a day. They didn't rush, they explained, because there was plenty of time to walk and plenty of time to rest.

Resting was not always a respected goal on the Camino. It was easy sometimes to forget that the walk is a pilgrimage and not the Boston Marathon. Many pilgrims approach it as a test of physical endurance, an athletic challenge whose greatest participants are those who walk thirty or more kilometers a day, every day, on the blistered balls of their feet, eating only sweet red peppers, spending less than ten pesetas a day, and finishing the whole thing from France to Santiago in less than three weeks. One day, as Alex and I walked downhill toward the little town we were staying in for the night, a squat and solidly built Frenchman with hairy legs squeezing out of tight red shorts caught up to us.

"How many kilometers did you walk today?" he shouted.

"Eighteen," I replied as he passed.

"Forty! I walked forty today and yet I will arrive in town before you!" His victorious fist pumped toward the sky as he strode off ahead of us and broke into song.

We threw our backpacks to the ground and sat down on the bench. Before long, it felt as though I had also sunk peacefully into the stones.

A young and pretty woman in a flowered blouse and blue skirt appeared. She held up a key and smiled. It always surprised me to see young people in the little towns along the way, as if the inhabitants of centuries-old buildings should themselves be centuries old. We followed her across the street to the door of a building I hadn't recognize as a church when we were sitting in front of it.

The interior of the church was an octagon, no more than twenty-five feet wide. The air had been turned golden and shining by millions of bits of dust lit by the sun. They floated in spirals on unfelt drafts.

No paintings or sculptures hung on the pale yellow walls. There were no pews and no stained glass. The only object breaking up the expanse of creamy gold, as though all that light and yellow stone were simply a stage for it, was a crucifix.

It was made of wood, about four feet high, painted in a high sheen. Jesus was emaciated, twisted, each muscle outlined by its shadow, a crown of thorns on his head, painted in pale yellows and white and browns that blended with the floor and walls.

Tiny red drops of blood erupted from each wound on the head, hands, feet, and abdomen. They ran down his face and neck, down chest and legs where they gathered on his toes in gumdrop-size blobs. They ran horizontally across his arms, and then veered down in sharp arcs. Red, bulbous, big fat drops of blood like rainwater just about to drop off an eave. They were perfectly shaped and perfectly spaced across the body, hanging off thin crimson lines of blood that trickled over torso and limbs. Bright red against soft gold.

I had seen other bloody crucifixes before, but this one mesmerized and frightened me. The crucifix should have been gruesome, but it wasn't. It was beautiful. The blood trickling and spurting from all over the twisted body was beautiful. In hundreds of red drops painted on this crucifix, each perfect in its fat and round symmetry, one could see that the unnamed medieval artist loved that blood—loved every drop he so carefully painted.

The fields surrounding the town, fields we had just been walking through, were the same colors as this crucifix—gold wheat and red poppies. Whenever I saw poppies floating on the wheat, I thought of blood. It was as though I had been walking through the crucified Christ, as though the land itself was Christ, as though He pulsed and breathed and grew all around me and I had not noticed until this crucifix made it obvious. It gave me the creeps. While walking the Camino, I felt pulled back to the faith I had known all my life, but on seeing that cross I was once again repelled and confused by the act at the very heart of it—violent and bloody. The unnamed artist had found a way to make the violence beautiful, and it frightened me.

"Come, come. I must get back to the shop, and you must be getting on your way. You said you wanted Cokes?" The shopkeeper ushered all of us back out into the blinding sunlight. Snapped out of one world—a world of beauty and violence and an unnamed artist's unmistakable love hanging on a wall for centuries, where I felt as though I was touching yet not grasping something, and thrust into another, a world of Coke cans and ice-cream sandwiches—I could not understand how these two worlds could exist at the same time and in the same place. Yet they did. I had to live in both at the same time, just as easily and seamlessly as the Spaniards around me seemed to, a world where red and gold is poppies and wheat and Coca-Cola bottles and blood and flesh.

6.

I've believed in God since I can remember. My parents told me God existed and that Jesus loved me, and because they said so, I believed it. I didn't think about it very much when I was little. Religion for me was the way the sun shone through the church windows casting blocks of color across the floor and my arms and legs, the roast beef and buttered carrots every Sunday on the fancy china, and my mother setting my straight hair in pin curls the night before my first Holy Communion. That was what being Catholic was, and that was somehow also what God was.

It's these types of experiences, religion of the everyday and religion in the home, that shape a person's faith and understanding, the historian of religion Robert Wuthnow argues. It isn't the theories about God learned in formal religious education or training that determine the depth of religious identity, but rather the mundane experiences of religion absorbed through the senses. Consequently, I was Catholic to the core.

In my all-girls Catholic high school, I first realized there were some problems. We took theology classes on the demand for social justice inherent in Catholicism, but then learned about the institutional injustices rife throughout the history of Christianity. Then again, there was Sister Rosina, the school cook who would first scold you and then fix you a turkey sandwich if she realized you were eating Ring Dings for lunch because you didn't like what she cooked that day. If religion confused me in the classroom, it made perfect sense in the cafeteria.

In college, adolescent doubts became flat-out confusion when I majored in religion. All the political maneuverings of the early Christians, the ways religions have been used to oppress people, the theories that argue that religions are tools for maintaining the status quo or the result of primitive people trying to cope with death, and the fact that other religions' explanations of reality make sense, too, and that millions of people believe those other religions just as strongly as I had mine—it was all so interesting, but all so disturbing. Was any part of any religion true, or even meaningful?

Even though my interest in religion grew and grew, leading me to divinity school, my faith didn't mature at all. It remained, as I think it does for a lot of people, at some mixture of a child believing what I was told, of knowing—similar to that absolute way a six-year-old knows Santa Claus will come Christmas eve—that the world works a certain way and that I could navigate happily and successfully through it, and the college freshman's shallow skepticism. Sure, God was there, but I didn't really have any need for God, except maybe to help out during final exams. And religion, well, religion was just a corrupt but fascinating human construction.

I think the crash into the living room couch after dad died was the result of realizing that none of what I believed in an unthinking, almost instinctual way, was accurate. But though my certainty of how the world worked was pulled out from under me, I had nothing with which to replace it. And so I fumbled through that year.

PART 2

Walking

7.

A pilgrimage starts the moment you pull the front door shut behind you. We met a few pilgrims from Belgium and Germany who walked the whole way, down their front paths and all the way to Santiago, and a very few who even planned to walk back, but for most modern pilgrims, cars, trains, and airplanes were some part of the journey from home to Santiago. Our pilgrimage began in a Green Cab of Somerville, swerving through the Ted Williams Tunnel to Logan Airport.

I'd read about package pilgrimage tours to places like Lourdes and Medjugorje, where it is clear from the moment you get to the airport and meet up with your tour group, put on your matching T-shirts, and share stories on the plane, that you are now a pilgrim. But for the first week of our trip, it didn't really occur to me that I was a pilgrim. I never had some liberating moment of realizing that I had entered a liminoid existence in which I was released from my everyday life and from society's expectations of me, or that my purpose in life had changed. This is, in part, because I spent the first few hours of my pilgrimage on the plane frantic that I had not attached the illustrations I had referred to in my last term paper, worrying that Alex had forgotten to pack something for me, and generally convinced that everything would go wrong. As soon as our dinner trays were cleared, I took five Tylenol PMs and knocked myself into a chemically induced sleep.

Or perhaps I never had that feeling of officially becoming a pilgrim, as someone travelling to Lourdes or Fátima might, because of the very nature of the pilgrimage to Santiago de Compostela. Christian pilgrimages can be divided into three broad categories. Santiago is a "medieval" pilgrimage; Lourdes and Fátima are "modern" ones. The third category, "archaic," refers to pilgrimage to places that have been considered holy for very, very long times, and through many different religions. The terms refer to the time period the pilgrimages developed, but they also refer to some specific characteristics of each.

A pilgrim on a modern pilgrimage may use modern means of transportation to get to the site—planes and trains and automobiles will take you almost right up to the grotto in Lourdes, with little walking or hardship. It is the *communitas* found at the site itself that is the focus of pilgrimage, not the pilgrim's arduous journey to it. But despite the modernity of travel, many aspects of modern pilgrimages seem quite antimodern—apparitions, miraculous healings, secrets, and apocalyptic messages about the end of the world and the evils of modern living. The focus on the *communitas* of the pilgrimage site, along with the stress on miracles that usurp the laws of medicine and science, make the modern pilgrimage a challenge to the predominant ideologies and social structures of today.

The medieval pilgrimage is quite different. It developed in a time when pilgrimage was a common part of life. It was not in opposition to the reigning times and was well-integrated with the social structures. There always remained something about it, though, the *communitas,* that eluded tight social control and therefore raised suspicion. For the medieval pilgrim, the journey itself was important because there was and is something transformative about walking for dozens and perhaps hundreds of miles with your belongings on your back. The medieval pilgrimages were more focused on the process of pilgrimage, on becoming and being a pilgrim, than on visions or miracles at the pilgrimage site. Even today, the focus of the pilgrimage to Santiago is on the journey itself and on the transformation of *becoming* a pilgrim over the course of the journey.

When we landed in Paris and Alex shook me awake from the soundest sleep of my life, we didn't know which of the four train stations we needed to go to. After driving by the Eiffel Tower in the tour bus a few times, panic began to rise through my legs and into my chest. (The taxi drivers were on strike, with the public transit workers striking in support, or perhaps vice versa—we never did figure it out—and the only way from the airport to the city was tour bus.)

"Alex, we have to get off the bus."

"We don't know where we're going yet."

"Please, Alex, we have to get off. Right now."

"Okay, okay. Just don't hit me with your shoe."

I have never hit Alex with my shoe, or anything else, but he sometimes says this as a way to tell me to calm down. This time it just pissed me off. I considered reaching for my shoelace.

We got off at the next stop. On the corner, just across the street, was the Gare de Sud, the right station. Our train was to leave in a half hour. It didn't make me feel any better.

"You always read of stories like this when people go on pilgrimages—where things all just fall into place. Maybe that's what just happened with us. I mean, it was pretty amazing that we just happened to get off the bus in front of the right train station in a city this big, don't you think? I think this is all going to work out fine," Alex said, turning his face to try to meet my eyes.

"Oh yeah, definitely," I said, avoiding his gaze. I didn't agree with him at all. I was surprised he knew anything about pilgrimage, and that he was willing to so easily ascribe our luck to a higher power.

We took the train to Bayonne and spent the night there before taking another train to Saint Jean. This train was really more of a mountain trolley than a train. It was only one car long, and the engine and the passenger compartment were in that same car. The engineer was also the conductor and the brakeman. He collected our tickets and closed the door, made the announcement, and then turned around and turned the trolley on. The ratcheting and wheezing of the little train made conversation with the other passengers impossible. The car hugged the sides of the mountains, so that through the left-side window all you could see was the blur of chipped granite or evergreens brushing the glass, but through the other side the view of the mountains opened more and more the higher we climbed, until we could see for miles through the chasms of the valleys and over the tops of the peaks. Small gray clouds floated along at eye level. The train twisted along the sides of mountains, steadily climbing higher into the Pyrenees, until it dropped us off at its only station stop, close to the Spanish border.

A wiry woman who was waiting for the train bounded over to us with a wide smile and asked if we needed a place to stay for the night. As soon as we dropped our bags at Maria's house, she ushered us back out the door. "Go, go, you must hurry to Madame de Bril's. She is just up the street. Number seventeen, but she eats her dinner soon. Go knock on her door. She will give you your *credenciales.* Go!"

Madame de Bril had lived on the Camino for many, many years, our little guidebook told us, and was one of the Amigos del

Camino who helped revitalize and reorganize the modern pilgrimage. Since Saint Jean was the town at the base of the pass over the Pyrenees where ancient pilgrims from northern and western Europe used to congregate before crossing into Spain, it became a natural starting point for modern pilgrims, the unofficial place where "the Camino" begins as distinct from all the other walking paths across Europe. Since Madame de Bril lived in this town, she became the unofficial christener of pilgrims. A *credenciale* from her is a blessing of sorts. Maria pushed us out the door to Madame's house with the same intensity she would use the next morning to wake us at five and get us out the door, full of fresh bread and butter and jam and strong coffee, by a quarter to six.

When we knocked on the door at number seventeen, a house flush up against the stone road, a stern woman wearing a blue sweater, knee-length black skirt, and eyeglasses opened the door, silently waved us in, turned her back, and walked inside. We followed her to a dim room stuffed with papers and books. She sat down at a cluttered desk under a window in the corner, where the fading light cast yellow shadows. Three other pilgrims were there already. As she finished up her gruff business with them, we stood and watched.

"You need *credenciales*?" she asked, turning to us suddenly. "Let me see your papers."

I had a nice letter of introduction, on Harvard letterhead and written in Spanish, explaining I was a theology student. This seemed to impress Madame de Bril. *"Teología!"* she exclaimed in Spanish. "Harvard!" she said even louder, but this time with a French accent. She flashed me a big smile. I had just witnessed her turn down a man, refusing to grant him a *credenciale* because she was not convinced he was in the right frame of mind and heart to be a pilgrim. Madame de Bril was known for being finicky about to whom she would give a *credenciale* with her name on it, our guidebook told us, so when she seemed so pleased with my letter, I thought I would be approved with no problem. But then she asked why I was doing this pilgrimage.

"Why?" I repeated. I had no idea why.

"Yes," she said. "What is your intention for the pilgrimage? I need to know. You must have a reason to do this. I need to make sure it is a good reason."

Throughout the history of Christianity, there have been many reasons people have gone on pilgrimage. Some went to fulfill a vow made to God. A person might have promised to go to Santiago if only her child, or husband, or mother survived an illness. These vows were not seen as meaningless bargain-making in a time of desperation, nor were they completely private. If a person could not fulfill her vow for some reason, she had to seek official church permission to be released from it, and often had to do something in place of what was promised. Others might have gone as penance. Sinners were often assigned to go on penitential pilgrimage in confession. The worse the sin, the farther the pilgrimage. Under the Bishop of Rochester, in England in 1325, a parishioner guilty of "disturbing the peace" only had to go to the local cathedral as a pilgrim, but the man who confessed to "adultery with godmother" was sent off to Santiago. In the late medieval age, even secular courts handed down pilgrimage as punishment. According to legal and church records, Santiago was a popular sentencing choice. Sometimes a pilgrim went to offer thanksgiving, and sometimes to ask for help or beg for a favor or seek healing. Henry VIII went to the shrine at Walsingham to ask God to give him a male heir. His intention famously went unfulfilled, and he later shut down all the shrines in England. You have to wonder if it wasn't at least a little bit out of spite. Sometimes, especially at the height of the medieval pilgrimage boom, people went to get the indulgences, which were offered with alarming frequency after the twelfth century. And sometimes people went on pilgrimage out of the desire to go to a place where God might just be a bit closer.

But I had none of those traditional intentions for walking the Camino, nor did I know of any of them as I stood before Madame de Bril.

"Well," my mind frantically searched for the reason why I was doing this, "my father died last June," I blurted out.

"Ahhh, of course," she said, satisfied. She clucked her tongue against the top of her mouth. "I am sorry, so sorry." She peered at me over the top of her glasses with sympathetic eyes and the tightly pressed half-smile people always give when you say your father died the year before.

That satisfied her? How could that satisfy her? But it did. In fact, it made perfect sense to her.

"And you?" she thrust her chin at Alex, all evidence of empathy carefully reigned back in.

Alex, who does not speak a word of Spanish or French, pointed at me. "Protector," he said matter-of-factly.

"Of course!" Madame de Bril said, delighted. With great pomp she stamped our passports and handed them back.

The man who was turned down just before us and had stayed to argue his cause was as baffled by her satisfaction as we were. He said his reason for doing the pilgrimage was that he wanted to experience the spirituality of the Camino. This reason—an unformed desire of a spiritual sort not connected to a particular religion—is the most common one that people give for doing the Camino today. He was flatly rejected. I was walking the Camino because my father died and Alex was doing it because he was afraid I'd be kidnapped by mimes or trampled by mad cows. Neither of our reasons seemed to have anything to do with God or spirituality or religion. The man began to argue, but she waved him off.

My answer at Madame de Bril's was the first time I made the connection between my father and the pilgrimage. I was not sure at the time that I meant it.

8.

In the early morning, the air and light matched the color of the stone buildings and streets. We walked under the archway next to the church and across the bridge, leaving Saint Jean as bells chimed six.

We walked and walked that day, up through the mountains as the sun came out and the sky turned blue. We followed the Route Napoleon, the road through the Pyrenees that Napoleon Bonaparte used, the same route Charlemagne's army marched, the route that Maria told us Hannibal tried to cross with elephants—with no success. The Camino was a paved one-lane road that twisted though pastures, marked with red and white blazes. As we climbed higher, we could see flocks of sheep like white dust on the green slopes far below us. Twice we passed shepherds working in the high pastures who cheered us on, and once when a car drove by the driver rolled down his window and shouted, "*Allez!*"

If one begins in Saint Jean, the first day of the Camino is the longest distance one has to walk in a single day. You pass the last lived-in home only a few miles after starting, and then have to walk many hours through uninhabited mountains until you reach the monastery at Roncesvalles, in Spain. On every other leg of the trip, the Camino passes through many little towns a day, and you can stop in any one you choose or need to stay in, but on this first day there is no choice but to push on and on for twenty-eight kilometers.

It felt good to walk, good to have a purpose and a destination after a year of not knowing what I was doing. I was going to Santiago de Compostela, and I knew exactly how I was going to get there. The way was well marked, millions had walked there before me, and Alex was going there, too. That night, we would stay at the monastery in Roncesvalles, where a *refugio* founded in the eleventh century is still open to pilgrims today. I sped ahead. My mind careened along with my body past streams and through meadows.

The Pyrenees were steep and jagged, but they didn't break into gray granite at the peaks. Instead they were green to the very tops, not with forest but with grass and fields. Scattered rock outcroppings appeared every now and again. Gentle meadows quickly dropped off into steep inclines, causing a dizzying vertigo when you looked straight down, then leveled off into more gently sloping meadows, sometimes with sheep and a man or two sitting there. This pattern continued all the way down to the valleys, where distant towns of white buildings and faded red roofs punctured the green. As high as these mountains felt, with steep and open peaks and unobstructed views of rows and rows of ranges, they did not feel at all isolated or intimidating, for villages speckled the view, and they were worked to the very tops, with shepherds using even the highest fields in the summers.

It was these shepherds, working so high up, in a place that seemed closer to heaven yet still firmly a part of the earth, who placed a statue of Mary on a rock outcropping overlooking a valley, at the edge of a steep grass slide.

IN NINTH GRADE, Miss Conlin pointed out that at the time Mary lived, she would have been betrothed in her early teens. She would have been, at the time of the annunciation and the birth of her son, just about the same age we were then, sitting in that theology classroom.

"Just imagine what happened to her," Miss Conlin said. "Just imagine if it were you. Imagine an angel shows up in your bedroom tonight. We know Mary was scared, because the first thing the angel said was 'Don't be afraid!' And then he says: 'God has chosen you—you, Mary—to do something very special, to be someone very special. God wants you to be the mother of the messiah! But he wants you to become pregnant now.'

"Now, Mary knew what this meant. She was a smart girl. She knew that Joseph would reject her if she turned up pregnant, because he'd know the child wasn't his. She knew that her family could disown her, she knew that she could be stoned for this. She knew that her very life was on the line. Imagine if you got pregnant and had to try to explain to your parents and your friends. What would you be thinking and feeling? And Mary had it even worse than you. She could be put out in the streets, destitute and starving.

"The angel was waiting for her answer. She could have said, 'No, I don't want this. Leave me alone!' She could have said no. And what did she say? Knowing what all this could mean, what did she say to God? She said *Yes*!"

Miss Conlin pointed her finger at us and scanned the classroom. "Could you say yes? Would you have that kind of courage? Do you have that kind of strength? Would you have the sheer guts to say yes if an angel showed up in your bedroom tonight?"

We sat in our seats, mesmerized, and shook our heads. No way, we wouldn't have that kind of courage.

"Well then, next time you are afraid to do what you know is right," Miss Conlin continued, "you think of Mary. And ask her to help you find the kind of strength and courage she had. She was the bravest, strongest, most daring person who ever lived."

WHEN I TOOK my first religion class in college, and learned that this image of Mary—Mary as the courageous firebrand risking everything to change the world, bucking the system, the model for throwing off the shackles of society's expectations and doing what your soul tells you to do—that this understanding of Mary was not the one encouraged for most of Christian history, nor even the most popular modern understanding of her, I was, at eighteen years of age, honestly shocked. I thought the "meek and mild" language from Christmas carols was just for alliterative effect. I didn't know that people actually saw her that way, and that some argue that this image of her was used for centuries to justify a subservient role for women in society.

So here she was again, on the Camino. The statue smiled sweetly down at us, her hands slightly spread open. It was the first of the hundreds of statues of Mary we saw in Spain—in churches, but also in meadows, on mountains, in miniature roadside shrines, in front of houses, in caves, on ancient and fading pillars to mark the route.

I wondered what the shepherds who placed her there thought of Mary, and why they wanted to have her there. For me, it felt like running into a friend when you least expect it.

THAT AFTERNOON I spent all my nervous energy and was left with out-of-shape legs, burning lungs, and two blisters that slowed us down considerably. It was growing dark as Alex and I made our way down the steep vestiges of a Roman road through an old chestnut orchard. The Romans apparently had no concept of switchbacks, and on this fourth long and steep downhill of the day we moved cautiously. I tried to convince myself it wouldn't be so bad to sleep out here tonight. I stopped looking for the monastery through the trees.

And then, suddenly, we heard voices, and a second later saw the massive stone building through the trees. We were there. It was a few minutes before eight o'clock.

A man in his forties, in street clothing, welcomed us through the wide front doors of the sprawling structure and commented that it was late, very late. He stamped our *credenciales* and sent us up to the dormitory, a large and airy room painted white with faded wood floors and long windows across the length of it that let in the sunset. A hundred bunk beds were scattered throughout.

As I sat down to take off my boots and put on sandals, Alex

went to wash his face and hands. I had just unlaced one boot when an older man, perhaps in his sixties, walked into the room and began to yell in Spanish.

"You are not supposed to be here! Out—you must get out. You have to go to Mass—it is starting downstairs in the chapel. Let's go! Let's go!"

I told him the man downstairs sent us up here just a minute ago. He didn't care. I asked if I could just have a minute to take off my boots to let the blisters get some air.

"I don't care what's wrong!" he continued to yell. "You must go to Mass!" He marched me downstairs triumphantly. I felt like a naughty six-year-old.

I stood in the back of the crowded chapel, stewing with disbelief and anger. I shoved my feet all the way forward in the boots, my toes scrunched up against the front, to try to give the raw and burning skin some room. Alex joined me a minute later, grinning, after he was discovered and accused of hiding in the bathroom.

"I can't believe this," I thought as I stared at the backs of the heads in front of me. "This is like Mass as punishment." I had such hopes for the pilgrimage, and that monk seemed to reinforce every bad stereotype of organized religion. He was more concerned that people show up at a ritual than that they are healthy or okay. I looked at my feet and bit my lips hard to keep from crying in anger. Making matters worse was that, in Spanish, the term used for "the Lord" is *el Señor*, and so as I listened to the ritual and tried to translate quickly in my mind, I kept thinking of God as "the mister." That really seemed to sum it all up for me right then, and the shameful treatment of and attitude toward women throughout Christian history flooded my mind. It was so easy to dismiss this uncaring, uncompassionate, rigid, male-run and male-dominated religion, one that set about to worship God as the ultimate man, the Mister. I snorted out loud.

When the time came for people to receive communion, everyone shifted, and I looked up. And there was Mary again—a small, smiling statue of her holding the infant Jesus above the altar. She looked amused.

"What do you think of all this, Mary?" I thought. And then I was startled to realize I was talking to Mary. I had not done that for years.

VERY LITTLE IS actually known about the woman who gave birth to Jesus. She appears just a handful of times in all four canonical gospels. Through the millennia, theologians, church leaders, and people who place her image in fields have developed all sorts of ideas about her, making Mary a symbol of something more, something else—a highly contested symbol.

Some have argued that the official complex doctrine surrounding Mary is a projection of a particular and odd understanding of what an ideal woman would be, as developed in the minds of a celibate, all-male hierarchy. These were men whose primary experiential knowledge of women, for the most part, was through relationships with their mothers, and not intimate, mature, loving relationships with women in adulthood. And so Mary is defined through virginity and motherhood, not as a person who, like any of us, is faced with a critical decision to do what she knows is right, in any area of life. Over time, for Catholics, she became an idealized über-mother, gentle, sweet, perfect in patience, love. But not strength or fire or courage. And sometimes, it seems, not a real woman who probably lost her temper when Jesus was late for dinner.

The Catholic Church also understands Mary as a symbol of the Church itself. Just as Mary is the *theotokos* (Greek for "God-bearer") for giving birth to Jesus and so bringing him into the world, so is the Church bringing the real presence of Christ into the world.

For many Protestants, Mary has also become a symbol, not of the sacramental power of the Catholic Church, or of perfect motherhood, but of what is wrong in Catholicism. Mary is one of the most divisive issues separating Catholics and Protestants today. The image and idea of Mary has come to represent not just the first-century Jewish peasant woman but a whole range of hopes, fears, ideals, and disagreements.

I wonder what Mary must be thinking all these centuries. What would it be like, after all, if people were to spend the next two thousand years discussing when and if you ever lost your virginity and whether your hymen broke while giving birth?

I don't know how the monks who put the statue of Mary in the chapel understood or envisioned her. All I know is that I was so relieved and happy, genuinely happy, to see her there, smiling at me, playing with her laughing baby. Mary would be popping up all over Spain, and I felt as though she was reaching out a hand to me, as though she were saying, I know they won't invite you in, but I will.

THE NEXT MORNING, as a kind Spanish doctor taped up my heels as best he could with the limited first-aid kit he found, a little old man came upstairs with a broom and began to reprove us in garbled Spanish, waving around his hands at the empty room and pointing to his watch. He would not stop yelling, no matter how fast I tried to pack up and hobble around in sandals. He began sweeping dirt at me.

"Damn old man! This is supposed to be a monk? What did I expect?"

Alex was waiting for me in the wide, stone hallway at the top of the steps. We walked down the faded, deeply worn wooden stairs. Just as we stepped out of the monastery, a younger man with a wide smile called to us from behind.

"What happened?" he asked, gesturing to my heels visible through the straps of my sandals. "Please, come with me."

He led us into a pantry off the kitchen, rummaged in the cupboard, and pulled out a small blue plastic box. This unassuming box held what was to become the most important item in my life during the pilgrimage—Compeed. I had never heard of the stuff or ever seen it before the Camino, but I became an ardent believer in the "hydro-seal cure" the little blue box promised. But I didn't become a believer that day, because even though the monk unwrapped the Compeed, and heated it up in his hands, and carefully placed it over my mangled heels, he didn't hold the little plastic bandage in place long enough, did not cup my bare foot in the palms of his hands as tightly as needed, and so was not able to secure the all important seal with his body heat. He sheepishly placed it on my bare skin, but then blushed deeply and dropped my foot. The plastic bandage fell off midway through the day. But that Compeed was healing nonetheless, a bit of spiritual healing in the kindness of someone who noticed my gauzed-up heels and tried to make it better.

9.

I didn't think I was hallucinating. No, I definitely saw something moving in the woods ahead of us. It seemed to be shaped like a human being, but it was too lumpy to be a person. It would appear on the trail ahead of us for just a few seconds, shrouded by the forest, and then disappear again for a few minutes. It was grunting and lurching and throwing its arms around. It wasn't walking like a pilgrim. But who besides pilgrims walked on this very isolated part of the Camino where it was more hiking trail than road, narrow and littered with big stones and tree roots, careening over rocky outcroppings? I began to wonder if I was seeing a Sasquatch. Was there such a thing as a Spanish Sasquatch? Or could I actually be seeing things? Had I completely lost my mind after just a day and a half walking?

But maybe it really was a person, a crazy person on the Camino. A giant, crazy person with an ax. I was keenly aware of and afraid of death after my dad died, without at the time being completely aware that I walked around with this fear. I was a champion worrier at this point in my life. I think that all the feelings I was holding off transformed themselves into anxiety. I worried so much it became physical. I twisted my hair constantly so that even if I wore it in a ponytail, I would absentmindedly pull out long strands to twist, so that by the end of the day, long ragged clumps of hair from different sections of my scalp would be flailing around my head while the rest of the hair was pulled back. I made two little bald spots where even today the hair grows in as soft, fine baby hair. I chewed on my lower lip at all times until it bled. When my lip inevitably became chapped I would pull off the flaky bits with my thumbnail. Alex, who could very reasonably have said, "Get away from me, you bleeding, balding, twisting, scratching miasma of worry," never said anything about it, except, perhaps, to point out when blood was trickling down my chin.

We were seeing the angry, grunting, misshapen creature more often, though it was no more discernible through the thick trees. Then we turned a corner on the trail, and there she was.

The short woman with soft black curls and dark liquid eyes threw a bag from above her head with a grunt, but it just ended up falling in the mud two feet in front of her and splattering her shins and shorts. She shoved the huge white puffy package she had wrapped around her waist bandolier-style to her back, creating a great bulge over her bottom. She grunted again and stamped her feet up and down in a little dance, punched the air, and pushed the sweaty hair from her face.

"Umm, do you need help?" I asked as we came up behind her.

"Oh God! No! I'm fine. Ha ha. Just fine. Ha ha. Ahhh." She smoothed down her T-shirt and rearranged the bundle around her waist in an attempt to make it look better. "I didn't realize anyone was there. I was just, you know, taking a little break." She answered us in English. "You two from the U.S.? You have American accents. Do you want some milk?" she asked, all the while still trying to pull herself together, tucking her hair behind her ears, kicking her bag in the mud closer to her feet. She bent down and extracted a cardboard container of milk from the bag.

"You're carrying around milk?" Alex asked.

"Well, that's part of the problem, the carrying part. Everything would be fine if the carrying part would work." She began to laugh.

Her name was Sylvia and she was from Florida, originally from Cuba. The large white bundle around her waist was her pillow, and the large bag she had tried to throw, and from which she extracted the carton of milk, was the cause of her problems. It was a convertible bag, one that changed from a backpack to a rolling suitcase.

She explained that she had thought it out, based on what she had read about the Camino and on her own limited experience of long-distance walking. She knew that because of a previous injury, her lower back and hips would eventually give her a lot of pain from carrying a backpack. She knew she liked suitcases on wheels. She knew that large stretches of the Camino were paved roads, where the ancient Roman roads and ninth-century farm roads that pilgrims once used to walk from town to town all the way to Santiago never fell out of use. Over the centuries, some of these roads were modernized. Some, through the evolution of transportation, had even become superhighways, where pilgrims incongruously troop alongside cars zooming by. (Luckily, the summer we were there, the government had begun to build dirt roads beside the superhighways, and plant trees along the way to provide shade. A pilgrim lane.)

"My theory was that on the paved surfaces, I could just wheel the suitcase along behind me, and on the rocky or muddy parts, I could carry it as a backpack. As you can see, it hasn't really worked out." She sighed.

Her plan turned out to be a disaster in practice. The bag was neither a comfortable and stable backpack nor an easily maneuverable and light pull-along suitcase. Because it lacked a hip belt that would shift the weight from her back and neck to her hips and butt, it cut deep into her shoulders. When Sylvia's back gave out that afternoon, she tried to wheel the thing on the rocky and fantastically muddy ground, but it only got about three inches before the wheels filled completely with mud that quickly hardened to a cementlike consistency.

She took a long drink from the carton and wiped her mouth with her hand. "Milk is my favorite thing," she said while offering the box to us. "Since the milk they sell here has been zapped, it doesn't go sour. Want some? It's not bad. Just a little warm." Alex and I both declined. She shrugged and kept drinking. "If I drink it all I won't have to carry it anymore."

We three set out together through the forest. Sylvia regaled us with stories from her life and told us every joke she knew. She laughed so hard at her own jokes that she sometimes had to stop walking just to catch her breath and wipe tears from her face. We sang songs we made up as we went along, with lyrics about her suitcase, which seemed to take on a life of its own, bounding and bouncing over the terrain. After a couple of miles, Sylvia decided to just heave the bag down the Camino and let it roll down the hills on its own, which it did much more effectively than when she tried to pull or carry it, and with no more damage than a good coating of mud. We struggled to the tops of rises and plopped down out of breath, passing around the carton of warm milk. We picked up rocks as we went and looked for fossils embedded in them. Alex found a couple, I didn't find any, but Sylvia found dozens, just as some people have a knack for seeing four-leaf clovers while others can look in the same place for hours and find none. Sylvia gave off energy the way the rest of us give off body odor.

The feeling of laughing so hard and for so long was surprising. I hadn't laughed like that since the day before my dad died, a rainy Saturday when my two brothers and sister and I played Monopoly in my parents' house and my mother made hot dogs on buttered toast for lunch, just like she did when we were very little. I think that day spent with Sylvia, singing, laughing, looking for fossils—such a contrast to what I had been doing for the past year—was when I began to understand just how odd and off I had been living. I realized I'd been numb for months.

By two o'clock Sylvia decided that she was going to ditch her bag, take a cab to Pamplona, and buy a backpack built for hiking and camping like ours, like all the other pilgrims but her seemed to have. By the time we arrived at town that evening, Sylvia decided what she really needed was a donkey, a strong and sturdy donkey. The guidelines of the Camino don't preclude pilgrims from using pack animals to carry their belongings.

We stumbled down the Camino as it descended rapidly and rockily to the town of Zubiri. When we reached the damp concrete *refugio,* Sylvia declared that after the day she had, she was staying in a hotel. This possibility hadn't occurred to Alex and me. We just assumed that being a pilgrim meant sleeping in a dormitory with dozens of other snoring pilgrims. We got a room with a private bath, declined a wake-up call for the next morning, and ate sausages and thick potato and onion omelets and asparagus and buttery steaks for dinner before collapsing on the beds to watch Spanish team handball on TV. Thus started a trend.

SYLVIA'S BAG WAS so heavy and cumbersome because she was carrying around a well-stocked first-aid kit. She was a nurse. Giving up the weight of the kit wasn't an option, because it was the purpose behind her pilgrimage. She had been in a terrible accident a few years earlier and had not been expected to live, but she did, against all odds and all predictions. This pilgrimage was her way of saying thank you, of giving back whatever she could to whomever she could in order to thank whatever it was that gave her the chance to live. She planned to help people along the Camino, to wrap ankles or splint knees or tweeze out splinters—or tend to blisters. Giving up was not an option, but she only had a limited amount of time to walk the pilgrimage. Finishing didn't seem important, nor seeing the beautiful or historical landmarks, nor earning a *Compostela*. But walking was, as was being available to whoever might need a nurse along the remote and isolated parts of the route. And so a donkey seemed like the answer.

At breakfast, Sylvia asked the waiter where she could find one to buy for the trip.

"Why do you want a donkey?" he asked.

"To help me carry my things. The rolling bag was a disaster, my back is sore, and I know you can use a donkey to carry your stuff. So I thought I'd buy one for the rest of the Camino."

"Oh, please don't do that. That is a very bad idea. Very bad idea," he repeated while looking at her intently, and vigorously shaking his head. "It will only cause you more trouble than carrying your things," the waiter said.

"But I could go farther and faster with a donkey."

"No, no! How many times have I seen it myself? Dealing with a donkey is more work than carrying your bag could ever be. Just a few weeks ago, two pilgrims with donkeys camped out behind the hotel, and they asked us where they could sell the animals. They couldn't take it anymore. They were ready to quit."

"Really?" she asked.

"If you have a donkey, you cannot stay in the *refugios*. Where will the donkey sleep? And you have to care for the donkey, feed him, clean his hooves, make sure he is doing well."

"Oh."

"And a donkey won't move when he doesn't want to. He will just plant his feet and bray. You'll have to tug and tug at him. Then you won't walk anywhere at all that day." He shook his head again and grabbed her hand. "I beg you not to buy a donkey!"

She decided against it.

I THINK A lot of people do something similar to what Sylvia did—develop a theory of how something should work that isn't necessarily based on experience. You may think it is, but when something happens to challenge this well-constructed premise, you realize just how much of it is based on what others have told you, or what you assumed, or what you dreamed up. It doesn't fit the reality of six-inch mud, and so then you have to adjust, or sometimes you have to start over. That disconnect between what you expect something to be like and plan for and the way that it actually happens, often in a way that seems to be spinning out of control, is sometimes just annoying, but it sometimes causes a flat-out spiritual crisis. And you never know what may or may not cause this for another person. People sometimes ask me if I ever get annoyed with some of the people I see as a chaplain—if I ever get frustrated or impatient with people who seem to be having a meltdown because their ninety-six-year-old grandmother died or their cat ran away. And they ask if it's hard to take them seriously when I also have to be with twenty-two-year-olds dying of cancer or someone who fell down the basement stairs and is paralyzed from the neck down. But it really isn't because no matter what causes it, the pain of a spiritual crisis is intense and terrifying.

I suspect that some people never go through one of these crises where they realize that their entire way of navigating through the world was based on assumptions or someone else's ideas, and that the things happening in their lives are making it impossible to hold on to that old way of being in the world. Maybe this is because nothing ever challenged their way of seeing the world, or perhaps they were able to make small and nuanced changes to deepen their ways of thinking as they went along, and so never had a meltdown. I don't know why some people bypass it. But if you have gone through such a time, or if you are going through it now, you might know that sometimes hearing another person's way of making sense of her story, even if it is nothing like your own, and then being able to say, yes, that makes sense to me, or no, I think she is wrong in believing that—it can help.

I KNEW A fair amount of theory in general when I began the pilgrimage, all gleaned from books. I knew theory about grieving, theory about pilgrimage, and I knew theory about God. I didn't have too much experience of God, or at least any I bothered to pay attention to and was able to recognize as the presence of God. And even though it was almost a year after dad died, I had staunchly held off the darkest part of grief. I didn't really know what either God or grief were, though I thought I did. It was through walking, eight or ten hours a day, that I first began to get a glimpse of either, and neither was what I expected.

10.

With a deep and obscene slurping sound, I yanked my foot from a pool of thick black mud. Little blobs of goo went flying off the toe and hit the trees and brambles intruding on the Camino. I put my foot down on the ground and it kept on sinking, down, and down, sliding into the mud, up to the top of the boot. As I shifted my weight all the way onto that still sinking foot, my ankle and then my whole leg and hips began to wobble from side to side, instinctively looking for a balancing point. While still unbalanced, my other heel started to lift slowly and stiffly. Once again, to keep from falling face first, I yanked my entire foot from the slop, lifting the whole instep and toe and its heavy burden of mud in one piece and lurched forward again, mud flying, foot sinking, ankle wobbling, hips swiveling, and arms flailing again, all in a desperate attempt to balance, until a moment later it began again.

Until, suddenly, I was on the ground, sideways, my whole right side from foot to cheek lying in the soft, cold mud.

"Are you having fun?" Alex asked from behind me.

We had left Zubiri that morning. The day before we walked around the little town, spent hours soaking our feet in the cold stream that ran by the hotel, and said good-bye to Sylvia, who was taking a cab to Pamplona in the afternoon, planning on buying a proper backpack, and promising to write us notes in the logbooks at *refugios* ahead.

It had rained heavily during the night but cleared as we finished breakfast. We crossed the medieval bridge back out of town, found the yellow arrows pointing us down the deeply shaded Camino, and started the day's walk.

A PILGRIM TO Santiago walks not just to a place but to relics. A relic is some physical object associated with a saint. The most common, and probably the weirdest to present-day sensibilities, are pieces of the body of a saint, usually bones.

Saints were human beings like us. But unlike us, they are now in paradise. They are a bridge between heaven and earth, between the living and God. In the first few centuries of Christianity, as the early Christians developed their own unique way of understanding the world, the lives and especially the deaths of the saints were seen as proof of the power and love of God. Many of the early saints died as martyrs, executed by the Romans in sometimes grisly ways for their beliefs. The second-century saints Perpetua and Felicity were thrown into the Roman coliseum to be trampled to death by an insane cow. They survived, though, and a centurion was then ordered to slit their throats. The young soldier lifted his sword to Perpetua's neck, but faltered, unable to kill her. Perpetua, worried that he would be severely punished for failing in his duty, gently guided his sword to her throat. The manner of the saints' deaths, showing great strength and peace in the midst of great suffering as martyrs, was seen as proof of the ultimate triumph over death promised to the Christian at the future resurrection of the dead, and the power of God.

Some early Christians grew attached to a particular saint, emulating the saint's life and asking the saint to intercede with God on their behalf, assuming that the saint in heaven had influence that they, sinners on earth, did not have with the Almighty. These relationships with patron saints in some ways mimicked the social and political institution of patron relationships of Rome, but now on an eternal level. As the attachment and affection early Christians felt for these martyrs and holy people grew, so, too, did the importance of their tombs and graves. Eventually, their bodies (or pieces of it) were believed to be loci of great power.

It's not just the modern person who might find the idea of venerating a finger, say, or a jawbone, uncomfortable and sort of bizarre. In the first few centuries of Christianity, many people found the rise of the importance of the tombs of Christian saints and their bodies to be not just odd but a breach of the proper separation between the living and the dead.

But others saw the relic as a refutation of the victory of death. The representation of relics, tiny little bones encased in gold, became tangible and visual negations of death. There was no moldering corpse to see, but rather jeweled artwork. The goodness of the saints in life and their proximity to God in paradise was understood to resound still in their bones. The Holy, that most transcendant of ideas, could be identified and located—encapsulated in a piece of a body.

Because relics were believed to be remarkably powerful, people wanted to be near them, perhaps hoping that the presence and power of God would somehow seep into their bones, too.

As the centuries progressed, relics were routinely stolen from shrines, and saints' bodies were disinterred to be chopped up into pieces which then spread across Europe. Teresa of Avila, a sixteenth-century Spanish mystic who was well known as a holy woman in her own time, died while visiting a convent in Alba. The nuns buried her right away and then sealed her grave with stones and mortar, ensuring that no one could steal her holy body from their little convent. They wanted it to stay put. Nine months later, Jeronimo

Gracian, a leader of the Discalced Carmelites movement which Teresa founded, arrived from Avila. He had Teresa exhumed from her grave. Her body was found incorruptible—it had not decayed in the nine months since she was buried, and the sweet smell of flowers emanated from her. This was seen as irrefutable proof that she was a saint. Gracian immediately sawed off her left hand and brought it back to Avila in a locked box. (Teresa's hand has had adventures all its own, spirited all over Europe for centuries during wars and sieges. Franco kept it next to his bed until he died. It finally came to rest in the Carmel of Ronda. You can see pictures of it on the Internet.) The religious and civil leaders of Avila decided that the rest of Teresa's body also belonged in Avila, and while the nuns of Alba were in chapel one night, they stole into the convent and dug up Teresa's body, giving the sisters a severed arm as a consolation. The nuns were not consoled and complained to the pope, who ordered that Teresa's body be returned to the convent in Alba.

Relics were desired because relics were power—a direct line to God. As potent symbols of ultimate power, this also gave them political power. In the earliest centuries of Christianity, the prestige of local bishoprics was determined by how many saints' tombs were located there. In medieval times, relics were given and received in the political power plays of kings and princes. So these little bits of bone encompassed both spiritual and political possibilities.

Today, you can buy relics on ebay.com. Really. There are thousands of relics in the world, and all are venerated as bringing the holy a bit closer, but most are not the focus of a pilgrimage. This is because few are believed to have healing or prayer-expediting powers, and it is the very rare miraculous relic that became the locus of great pilgrimages, pulling millions of people across a continent, walking on roads like the one Alex and I were on.

THAT MORNING A few dark gray clouds like furry, slow-moving bears still hung low in the valley, trapped by the high mountains. The day was overcast, cool, and drizzly.

The Camino had been muddy before, but the heavy rains of the preceding night had turned the everyday sort of mud into a ribbon of shiny black muck six inches deep that stretched on for miles, leading us past fields and pastures of horses, slurping up rocks, tree roots, and probably small animals into its grasping, enveloping muddiness. It looked like it should be moving on its own like a river, but it only sprang into movement when touched.

Every step in this mud took complete concentration, and the focus on the sliding and shifting earth blocked out all other thoughts. It was fun to slide around in the mud like a little kid again, to listen to the sounds it made, to watch the mud fly through the air and smack into a vine and send it swinging, to feel the mud pulling. It almost felt alive, like an organism clinging to me, trying to hold me in as I stumbled through it.

THE ACT OF walking is, at the heart of the motion, falling. You pick one foot up off the floor and then must shift the bulk of your weight and center of gravity to that foot before it ever hits the ground, before it has landed on a secure footing. The crux of walking, the action that actually propels you forward, is a precarious one, an action in which you must move with faith that your leading foot will land on solid and even ground, else you might fall. For a second in every step, you are completely off-balance. Physical therapists tell patients who have to learn to walk again that it is "a controlled fall." You can see this when watching a baby learn to walk—the flat-footed lurch, all the weight transferred in a gamble to go forward. You could not stay in mid-step position, that point at which your weight has shifted, even if you wanted to. You can't hold it. The law of gravity says you have to fall once you make the shift that moves you forward.

In the mud, the fall wasn't as controlled as I was used to, and as I would have liked, and so I was much more aware of what my legs and feet and arms were doing than I normally would have been. I walked, both held back by the mud, and conversely, propelled forward by it, as deeply aware of my body as I had ever been.

RELICS ARE ABOUT the body—the saint's body, your body, the Body of Christ. Relics say that the body is not only important to God, but that the body is important in one's spiritual life. Their development as a cult object is a challenge to the neo-Platonic split of body and soul so often associated with Christian spirituality. Relics say that the human being is supposed to be body and soul together.

A relic points to the future resurrection of the body. This is the belief, a little bit wacky but massively important since the beginning of Christianity, that at some point in the future, after the Second Coming of Jesus, all believers' bodies will be *physically* resurrected, the same way that Jesus was physically, bodily, resurrected from the dead. In the future, all bodies will rise up from the grave and be restored to the way they were in life, but perfected, and the soul will rejoin that physical body in the Kingdom of God.

On the one hand, it's pretty hard to imagine millions of

corpses busting through the dirt like mummies from a horror movie. Bodies decay. Wouldn't the stink be unbearable? And how would all those billions and billions of people fit on earth? Traffic would be a nightmare.

On the other hand, if you suspend your common sense and rational disbelief for just a minute, and take seriously what this idea is saying about human beings, Jesus, and paradise, it can be a radical challenge to how many people understand themselves. In the Kingdom of God, that state of perfection when all is just as it should be on earth, human beings will be souls and bodies entwined completely, never to be severed again. *That* is how we are perfect. *That* is the triumph over death promised by the resurrection. *That* is how we will know God fully and joyously and completely. The body is not the enemy of the soul, as has so sadly been believed by even some of the saints whose bones are revered. The soul needs the body, and the body needs the soul, for it is through both together that one can come to try to know a little bit more about God.

The holiness of a saint—her willingness to be close to God, to seek and do God's will in this world—is not just in her soul. The holiness of a saint is in her bones, too. And at some point, that bit of bone will recombine with the soul in heaven. In this way, the relic collapses time right in front of the viewer. The past of the saint's miraculous life and death, the present of the viewer gazing on the relic, and future of the resurrection when those bones will live again are all collapsed into one tiny bit of matter, like a spiritual black hole.

Relics say that holiness can be located in an object or place. Some tombs of the saints were inscribed *Hic locus est*, Here is the place. But this idea is challenged by another, because by all appearances, holiness spreads. The cult of relics started with the tombs of saints. Then it became body parts, then to anything that had touched the living saint, and finally to anything that had touched the relic. Holiness can seep into other objects. In a survey ordered of all the villages of New Castile by King Philip in the late sixteenth century, the respondents in the town of Almoguera reported that when the bones of Saint Christopher were dipped in water, this water became healing, miraculous, and holy. In another town, the bones of a holy woman (not even an "official saint") were pressed against the skin of women struggling in childbirth in order that the baby about to be born come quickly. It's as though the presence of God, hovering around and in those bones, could be soaked out. The presence of God . . . holiness . . . grace . . . *something* is in those relics, but that something cannot be contained. It leaps out into anything that brushes it.

I THINK IT can't be a coincidence that relics lead to walking and vice versa. Walking, in its toll on the feet and back, and relics, in their grim, gray boniness, both lead one into considering the connection between body and soul. Relics and walking do the same thing; they tell us that it is through the *embodied* soul that we can come to know something about God.

LATER IN THE trip, during Mass at the monastery in Samos, the priest pulled out a giant silver reliquary with a brown bone behind a round window. Everyone lined up and walked to the front of the chapel to kiss the relic. After each kiss, the priest carefully wiped the glass with a cloth. The juxtaposition of modern sensibilities on hygiene and the archaic ritual of kissing body parts seemed not only absurd but also spooky and somehow unnatural, or supernatural. I stayed bolted in my seat, expecting to see ghosts rise from the dark alcoves or clouds of locusts burst through the doors. A friend from the Camino, an Irish girl in her early twenties, went up and kissed it. I asked her why afterward, and she answered, "Why not?"

Now I wish I had gone up there, too. Because why not? I can't say that I know how God works, or what holiness is, or how goodness flows. Maybe kissing saints' bones helps, maybe some presence of God would have seeped into me, as some believe it seeps into water and scraps of fabric.

WHEN WE STOPPED for a snack, sitting on two big boulders next to the path, I dropped a slice of orange. The pale orange and white lace veins outlined the crescent against the dark ground. When I looked down again fifteen seconds later, three giant black slugs, six inches long, were converging on the slice. They, lucky slugs, had no trouble getting through the mud, moving with surprising speed and grace. When the first of them got to the slice, two black pieces of slug flesh, looking like fangs, sank into the orange, and slowly and methodically started tearing it to pieces. By the time the two other slugs got there, the first had made a noticeable dent. You could see that he was eating the orange, not by anything he did, because he didn't seem to move very much, but by the fact that the smooth crescent outline was rapidly becoming ragged and frayed. His friends joined him on the other side of the slice, their long, pronglike mouths also fastened onto the orange, delicately ripping it to shreds. I shouted to Alex to look as another half dozen giant black slugs were converging. Within a minute, the entire orange slice was gone. All that was left were the gray-white seeds.

Every time we stopped to eat oranges after that, we dropped a slice on the ground and waited.

AFTER A FEW hours in which we walked only three miles, the low, bright green cover opened up, and ahead a low-slung, warm gray town stood in a field.

Roses were blooming all over the buildings of the town. They climbed and covered entire houses with hot pink flowers. Doors and windows barely peeped through the vines drooping with heavy blooms. The sky was still dark gray, and it made the fuchsia flowers all the brighter and more startling against the stone buildings. The humid air carried the scent everywhere. Our guidebook said that the mayor of the town strongly supports the Camino and pilgrims, and will stamp your *credenciale* in the town hall with his own *cello.* We walked through the town toward the town hall.

A woman sweeping her walkway laughed when she saw us caked in mud, and pointed us in the right direction. We were not more than two steps into the building when a middle-aged man warmly and rapidly greeted us and told us to stay right there, not to move, not another step, just stay right there. He would come over to us.

We waited in the black-and-white marble lobby and watched as the mayor carefully stamped our pilgrim's passports. He turned to a spool behind his desk and ripped off long pieces of yellow plastic ribbon.

"Please," he said, as he came back with our *credenciales* and the plastic, "let me tie these to your bags. They will warn the cars of your presence. They will be able to see these from a long distance. They will keep you safe as you walk on the highway." He knotted the long yellow plastic strips, which had "Camino de Santiago" printed in blue on them, resembling the caution tape police and firefighters put up to keep crowds away, onto our backpacks. The ribbon fluttering off Alex's backpack looked festive in the bleak day, even though it made him look like a crime scene.

"Now, please, don't go back the way you came," the mayor said. "You don't have to walk down that dirt road. You can take this paved road right out of town. It will take you to the next town, and you won't have to deal with all that mud. It will be much faster, much easier. Nice and clean. Just straight down this way." He pointed us down the road through town out to the highway.

I understood why he gave us the caution tape. The road was a highway with eighteen-wheel trucks rumbling by and cars zipping around them with only a narrow shoulder to walk on. We set off down the highway, and four seconds later I was afraid. At every crossroad we came to, I peered down to the left to see if I could catch a glimpse of the mud path, looking for the yellow arrows that marked the way on the Camino, but I didn't see any. The walking was easier on the body and the balance on the paved road, but harder on the mind. Grimy water flew off car tires and coated my face, and instead of bones sinking into the soft welcoming ground and hands brushing wet leaves, I felt afraid of the world.

I WANTED TO walk in the mud. I liked it. I liked sloshing around and slipping and falling and sliding. I liked that I could become filthy dirty. I liked watching and waiting for the slugs, and I liked the freedom.

As the wind from the tractor-trailers racing by blew the yellow plastic ribbon into my eyes and my resentment of the drivers and the mayor and the autoworkers who built all these cars grew, I realized with a jolt that part of the reason I was so happy walking in the mud was that I knew someone who couldn't. The last few years of his life, my father didn't really walk so much as he shuffled through the house in his slippers, unable to lift his gangrened feet from the ground. His toes turned black and the flesh fell off in chunks. I could not stand to think about my father's feet. I simply couldn't stand to think about it, as though my brain would split into pieces if I didn't get the picture of them out of my head, and a hot surge of panic welled up in my gut and chest and arms. I shook and swatted at the air in front of me with my hands, as though to shake the memory out of my body and push it far, far away.

MAYBE BECAUSE THE action of walking so closely mimics the action of prayer that it was through walking hours and hours a day that a new awareness of God began. Just like walking, prayer is the state of being off-balance—of moving, of not being able to stay in one place even if you want to because some force of nature won't allow it. This growing awareness of an odd thing you sense in yourself and around you may make you curious and hopeful, or it may frighten you and make you close down, shut off. But once the awareness takes hold, you will not stay in the same place. It will change and you will be off-balance.

The most effective way of moving depends on falling. A controlled fall, yes, but still a momentary loss of control—powerlessness, nonetheless. This can be frightening and damaging, no doubt—the fall that makes someone break her hip, or the fall into realizing the world cannot be explained with the tidy, neat explanations you have carried around. The fall into not-knowing, into realizing how little you know and how much more mysterious the world is than you thought. The fall into insecurity. The fall into regret, sorrow, despair, desperation. These are all frightening, terrifying, and yet they can still be moving forward. Or they can be falling down in the mud. But without taking the chance, you can't move at all.

The fall into prayer and the fall into grieving happened together, and both began in walking. Though I wouldn't have called that burgeoning awareness "prayer" just then. That understanding of it only came later. At first, I was just amazed at the peace I sometimes felt.

PART 3

Breathing

11.

Near the top of a long and steady climb up a ridge, a tiny spring bubbled out of the rock. This wouldn't have been anything remarkable just a few days earlier when we were still walking downhill through the wetness of Navarra, but after a few miles through the countryside just beyond Pamplona, it was a singular sight. The hill was a wide, rocky field dotted with struggling tufts of weeds burning in the mid-morning sun. Nothing grew taller than one's calf in the dry and sandy dirt. It was hot. It had been warm and humid before, but this was altogether different. The rocks and crabgrass shimmered in the heat. Alex and I hadn't packed enough water, and by the time we passed the ancient spring, my throat was burning. I could believe the legend that an exhausted and parched pilgrim had been tempted to sell his soul to the devil on that spot in exchange for a drink of water.

The pilgrim, many centuries ago, had also straggled up that baking hill, and had also run out of water. Just as he thought he couldn't move another foot, just as he collapsed onto his knees and thought his head was about to explode, a stranger appeared. But this was no Good Samaritan. It was the Devil himself in the guise of a fellow pilgrim, offering the dehydrated pilgrim cool, clean water if only he would renounce Jesus and the Virgin Mary.

"Never!" gasped the pilgrim, weak and close to death. "I would rather roast to death than renounce my Savior and Mother!"

"You fool!" Satan cackled.

But just then, so the little plaque bolted to the rock says, Saint

James himself appeared on his mighty white charger. He struck the ground, and out bubbled the coldest, purest, tastiest water anyone had ever drunk. The spring saved the faithful pilgrim. Satan was vanquished once again.

"I wish Saint James would show up right now. I don't even want a spring. Just a bottle of water would be good," Alex said.

"Saint James would never show up for us."

"Why not?"

"I don't know. He might show up for you. Actually, he probably would show up for you, because you're a good person. But not for me."

"What the hell are you talking about?"

"I don't know. I just . . . I don't know. Besides, I don't really believe that the devil appeared to a pilgrim and that Saint James showed up on a giant horse and whacked the ground and made a spring burst from the rock. So it doesn't matter."

Alex gave me a funny look. I was hoping that he would say something like, "Oh Kerry of course Saint James would show up for you, and probably even bring you ice cream, because you're such a good person. In fact, you're the most wonderful person I know. I love you completely." But he knew that if he said anything like that, I would argue with him till he gave up. He'd learned that the only safe response was a wrinkled nose and a raised eyebrow.

There was something comforting, standing on that hill, in realizing that we were not the only people to be thirsty and discouraged, in realizing that millions of people had walked this way before, with the same goal, and perhaps even the same doubts. Reminders of the modern pilgrim's relationship and continuity with the past are everywhere along the Camino.

This is a field that millions of people have passed before you, this is a fountain that people have drunk from since Roman times. Those ruts in the stone paving were made by thousands of iron wagon wheels trundling along, and in this church people have fallen to their knees and prayed for a thousand years. Someone else was hot and tired and thirsty and overwhelmed before you.

IT'S BELIEVED THAT the pilgrimage to Santiago began in the ninth century. The first records of Italian and French pilgrims come from the early tenth century. In the twelfth century, the French priest Aymeric Picaud wrote a guide for pilgrims, now known as the *Codex Calixtus*. Aymeric hated Spain with all his heart—hated the food, the wine, the landscape, the people, the weather. But his detailed guide gives a fascinating description of pilgrim life in the medieval ages, and helped spur on the explosive growth of the pilgrimage to Santiago de Compostela. As the pilgrimage to Santiago spread across western Europe, the impact of the Camino on art, literature, economy, and social customs grew and spread along with returning pilgrims. The danger to pilgrims also grew.

The most pressing dangers for modern pilgrims are probably hangovers from plentiful cheap red wine and the temptation of taking a train to the beach. Pilgrims of centuries ago had to contend with bandits, swindlers, wild dogs, filthy water, and fatal diseases. Death while away on pilgrimage was a real possibility, as medieval wills written out specifically for those on pilgrimage show. Pilgrims often banded together for safety, like those in Chaucer's *Canterbury Tales.* To go on a pilgrimage then was no light matter. Why would anyone go? Those on penitential pilgrimages had no choice, but for some, the promise of indulgences was the great motivator.

You can actually still get a plenary indulgence for making pilgrimage to Santiago today. Alex likes to show people his *Compostela,* the certificate proving one has made the journey, and tell them that it's his indulgence, a coupon from the pope guaranteeing him entry to heaven. Since it's written in swirling, calligraphed Latin, most people can't read it. They just nod solemnly.

Indulgences are much misunderstood. They are not Get Out of Hell Free cards, nor are they paperwork you bring with you when you die to guarantee that you get into heaven. They are an attempt (often quite flawed) to make tangible a complex theological idea.

Before 1100, it seems that "indulgence" had a more general meaning as forgiveness, but over time it came to mean remittance granted for penance due. And this is the crux of much confusion over indulgences, I think. An indulgence remits penance due, *not guilt.* For a medieval pilgrim, the guilt of a sin was understood to be forgiven by God through confession to a priest and absolution. Penance, however, or punishment due for the sin, was still needed, even after forgiveness was granted. An indulgence, then, forgives that need to do penance. It covered a specific amount of time and was given for completing some specific spiritual task. One still had to ask for forgiveness from God, and one still had to be truly contrite over one's sins, but with an indulgence, the penance owed was remitted. An indulgence could be earned by a variety of spiritual tasks, such as saying prayers, fasting, giving alms, or going on pilgrimage. For visiting a shrine, one might receive an indulgence of, say, fifteen days of penance due for the many sins a medieval person might be committing. Shrines had a set amount of indulgence given for visiting, and so relics and churches began to have quantifiable powers of salvation. The more difficult the spiritual task, the more of an indulgence one would receive. There was a close correlation between the difficulty, and one would assume, therefore, the transformative and reformative effects of a task, and the amount of penance remitted. Soon, though, this correlation would be cleaved, by the best of intentions.

Indulgences were important in medieval religious life because, it seems from the theological and pastoral handbooks that have survived from that time, medieval people lived in a world where the possibility and probability of sin lurked everywhere, ready to leap out and drag you down. Even the simplest requirements and joys of daily life were fraught with the danger of sin. And sin unpaid for through acts of penance led to Purgatory, a horrible, hellish state after death where one's soul would be cleansed of the effects of wrongdoing before admittance into heaven. If one earned enough indulgences, one could bypass this terrible and much feared state.

In 1343, Pope Clement VI wrote a bull explaining the theology behind what he called the Treasury of Merits, in part to try to clear some of the misunderstandings that were proliferating. Lots of false documents and rumors were floating around, claiming wildly generous indulgences. A popular misconception was that an indulgence covered one's guilt as well, allowing one to knowingly and willingly do as many bad and cruel things as one wanted, but this was not the case. Misunderstanding was enormous, perhaps because the anxiety about sinfulness was enormous.

As is usually the case, it is much easier to know what the "official" theological teaching was. It is a bit harder to discern what most medieval Christians believed, and how the idea of indulgences fit into their own attempts to make sense of good and evil, human weaknesses and guilt and God's forgiveness, and the priest's or the hierarchical church's role in that. But it is pretty clear that many of them—hundreds of thousands of them—wanted indulgences.

AT THE TOP of the ridge, giant medieval pilgrims in iron silhouette, walking and on horseback, men and women, rusted and weathered, stretched along the Camino as though walking next to us. It was a huge metal sculpture, fifteen feet high and fifty feet long, spread across the crest.

Catholic pilgrimage is, by its nature, both an internal, personal spiritual exercise and a deeply social action, its spiritual meaning embedded within and only possible through the larger community of the Church. One walks with other pilgrims in the present day, but also with all the saints and people of the past. We are all connected across time. Just as holiness seems to seep, so, too, it is believed, do the benefits of private spiritual exercise. Indulgences can be earned for other people; prayer can affect the fate of the dead. One asks a saint to pray for her because it is believed that the saint's prayer (or the prayer of anyone, for that matter) can effectively change one's heart and life, that prayer can literally change the world.

THE FIRST PLENARY indulgence was issued in 1300 for those who visited the Roman basilicas during the Jubilee year. Foreigners had to visit the churches every day for fifteen days, while locals had to visit for thirty. This special type of indulgence grants remittance of all penance due for everything ever done up to that point in life. The slate is wiped clean.

This was very popular. So popular, in fact, that people cried out that it was not fair that a plenary indulgence would be offered only in a Jubilee year—once a century. What about all those people born in 1302? It didn't seem likely that they'd be able to make a pilgrimage at the age of ninety-eight to get a plenary indulgence. The popes began declaring plenary indulgences much more frequently. But what about those people who had made a vow to go on pilgrimage but could not? For example, a list of dispensations granted by Pope John XXII in 1331 to people who had made vows to go on pilgrimage to Compostela tells the story of Hugh de Boville, a knight of the diocese of Sens: "When his wife, Marguerite de Barri was gravely ill, [he] uttered a vow that if she was cured of that grave sickness, they would visit the shrine of the blessed apostle James together, and Marguerite consented; but the aforesaid Marguerite, weighed down both by many childbirths (about twenty) and by the fact that she is getting on in years, and is in too delicate a state, cannot fulfill this vow. . . ."

Twenty childbirths. The woman must have been exhausted. In order to give people like Marguerite another option, the church allowed her to do other "works of piety." A good idea, and a kind idea, I think. A woman like Marguerite could receive the same indulgence she would have for going on the pilgrimage if she said prayers, gave alms to the poor, fasted, or if she paid for someone to do the pilgrimage for her. A gentle solution for those too weak to make a pilgrimage.

But it does mean that a wedge began to be driven between the actual transformative experience of going on a pilgrimage and the spiritual benefits. Over time, it was not just the weak who could pay for others to go on pilgrimage and give alms at a shrine in their stead, but those who simply didn't want to do it. People would go on pilgrimage in order to "transfer" the indulgence to someone else. Pilgrimage took on a vicarious power. Once started down this path, it wasn't long before people were just paying money in order to get indulgences. Couple that with the widespread misunderstanding about what exactly indulgences forgive (penance due, not guilt) and you degenerate into people believing they can "buy forgiveness." And, voilà—Martin Luther and the beginning of the Reformation. Well, actually, there was much more to the Reformation than that, but this is an attempt at the history of indulgences in a nutshell, and Luther's anger about the abuse of indulgences and his grave concerns about the theology of penance and the nature of forgiveness were at the heart of his ninety-five theses, the document that set into motion changes that created the modern Western world.

STRETCHING DOWN PAST the sculpture, along the long ridgeline, wind turbines twirled in the steady wind rushing up over the hill. Millions of pilgrims stood in the same wind, struggled to breathe as the same air caught in the backs of their throats as it did in mine. The rust-red and faceless pilgrims marched through time, for all time.

Perhaps the practice of indulgences in the high medieval ages, the time of the greatest popularity of the pilgrimage to Santiago, was deeply flawed. Still, there's something lurking there in the ideas behind the practice that I like—this idea of the seeping quality of spiritual work between people. If holiness can seep, so perhaps can the benefits of the struggle to understand what exactly that holiness is. We can help each other out. I can pray for all those past pilgrims, and they can pray for me, because we are not so distinct and separate as it might seem on the surface. We are all a part of this most private and most public experience of pilgrimage.

THE PILGRIMAGE TO Santiago de Compostela remained wildly popular for centuries, but then, slowly but surely, the

Camino fell on hard times. As the importance of images as centers for devotion increased, and the political climate of Europe underwent massive changes, the pilgrimage to Santiago fell out of favor. It's possible that the growing accessibility of earning indulgences in ways much easier than trekking across a continent in sandals also helped decrease the importance of the pilgrimage. By the sixteenth century, in that survey of Castilian towns, Santiago is not listed as one of the most important pilgrimage sites in Spain.

By the beginning of the twentieth century, it was almost impossible to find or identify the original route. An American art historian named Georgiana King set out in the midst of World War I to retrace the Camino. She was primarily interested in tracking the spread of Romanesque architecture along pilgrimage routes. She used the *Codex Calixtus* to retrace the way, which had been grown over and all but forgotten except by the people who lived along it.

In the middle of the last century, a young priest named Elías San Pedro Valiña was assigned a parish in a tiny town along the way. He took an interest in the old Camino. Also using the *Codex Calixtus*, he began to reconstruct the original route, finding the old wells, churches, and standing crosses mentioned in the codex. He bushwhacked his way through the overgrowth, freeing the roads. He marked the route by painting yellow arrows on rocks, trees, or the ground. Then something remarkable happened. Once way-marked, people began walking the Camino again, following the arrows pointing to Santiago. The Camino is a living pilgrimage again, with modern pilgrims journeying sometimes on the old Roman roads, some of which have sunk five or more feet below the level of the surrounding fields but with their smooth engineering still intact, sometimes dusty dirt roads, and sometimes on paved highways complete with road signs warning of "pil-grims crossing."

By the end of the Camino, close to Santiago, some pilgrims complained that the route was too crowded, that there were just too many pilgrims, not realizing that the Camino had, in its medieval heyday, supported many times the number who walked the summer of 1999. It is not that the route itself was too crowded, but that there were not enough places to sleep, not enough restaurants to support all the pilgrims. The towns cannot keep up with the exploding number of pilgrims, who once again just keep coming and coming and coming.

12.

The mud and roses of the Basque country gave way to wheat and vineyards and olive tree orchards after Pamplona. The colors changed from leaf green, pink, and chocolate to gold, olive, and white. As the landscape changed, so did the walking; the flat and dry ground meant I didn't need to concentrate on staying upright. Staring at the gentle hills on the horizon, my arms and legs swung back and forth on their own. Next to me, Alex sang a song to the tune of "Wanted, Dead or Alive."

> And I walk this road
> All the ladies want my hog
> It's so gigantic
> It's like a redwood log

I'm sexy
I come from a Texas town
I love all the ladies
And I never let them down.

He turned toward me and grinned.

"I didn't know you were such a fan of Bon Jovi."

"Oh, no, I'm not, but that one song is brilliant. Okay, it's your turn," he demanded.

"I can't."

"Yes you can. Just make up words as you go. Give it a try."

"There's no way I can beat that. Why try?"

"Come on. It'll be fun.

"Um, okay. Ahhh . . . I can't do this. I don't know how to start. I don't know what to say."

"Just sing about yourself. If you put it to a Woody Guthrie tune it's easier to make up words. Like for the tune of 'Jesus Christ,' you could sing:

Kerry was a girl,
A hard walking girl,
A hard walking girl and smelly
When Kerry walked through Spain,
All she talked about was foot pain
Till Kerry got to see Saint James."

He looked at me, waiting. I shrugged and held out my hands.

"Okay, try it to 'This Land Is Your Land.' You could start with, 'My name is Kerry; I am so hairy—' "

"I'm not hairy! And Kerry doesn't rhyme with hairy."

"Well, then you make something up."

> "My name is Kerry
> I like raspberries
> Umm . . . I am very hot now
> I hope we get to that town
> And that they have ice cream
> Ahhhh . . . And that I can eat it
> This land was made for you and me."

"That was really good!"

I looked at him and raised my eyebrows.

"No, it really was. You just have to keep trying." He launched into another song.

And so it went day after day. Early in the morning as we started walking, we talked about the towns we went through and the people we met. As the sun rose higher in the sky, we switched to singing, as pilgrims have done for centuries before us. When it got too hot to make up our own lyrics, we sang songs we already knew. In the late morning or early afternoon, when the sun shone down directly on our heads, we suddenly stopped singing or talking and trooped along in silence, our footsteps in tandem. I thought about dinner and how much I missed good pizza. I worried about what I would do when I graduated. I worried about my mother, my siblings, and whether or not Alex really liked me. I practiced Spanish in my head. Soon, as the grapevines and wheat began to shine white in the sun, it became too hot to think coherently. The heat, like a brick, would drop into the middle of a thought, cutting it off and leaving me confused and dizzy. It was as though the ability to think was leaking out through my pores along with sweat.

At that point, I watched my feet. I watched the way the boots made puddles of dust when they hit the ground, the way the shin muscles would bulge out with every step. I noticed the way my legs and arms and lungs all seemed to work together in their own pattern, without me even trying to coordinate them. Breathing in and out loudly to correspond with my steps hitting the ground made a nice rhythmic music. Breath came from both my belly and face at the same time, not my chest as I had always thought. An expanding feeling started by the belly button, and moved quickly up to my chest at the very same time that air came in through my nose to the back of my head. The air met the expansion deep in my rib cage, which seemed to rise up as my belly pushed out. Then it reversed. After exhaling, there was a long and peaceful pause when it felt as though everything had gently stopped. It wasn't at all how I thought breathing worked. Soon, I stopped noticing what it felt like, and without meaning to, I began to count my breath, "One, two, three, four." Two steps for every breath in and two for every exhalation. After a while the counting stopped. I just walked and breathed and listened to the sounds. I wasn't deep in thought; I was deep in nonthought.

I had learned walking meditation without trying. I'm not sure a pilgrim really has a choice. The physical demands of pilgrimage—the long miles, repetitive landscape, the crushing heat, the rhythym of walking for hours—all this allowed me to learn to meditate deeply and for long, long periods.

BREATH IS A miraculous thing when you have five weeks to notice it for several hours each day. Breathing can feel so good, filling a deep yearning for a sense of yourself, your own body, for connection with the world and the air around you. Breathing sustains us and allows us to live, yet we can go for days without even noticing it. Once the world has been shaken up a bit, once things are no longer on an even keel, breath comes crashing back into focus. "Take a deep breath," you tell someone who is upset, for conscious breathing can restore some sense of order and meaning.

Breath is one of the few functions of the body that can be both conscious and unconscious. Your body will continue to breathe until death even if you never think about it. But you can also choose how you breathe; you can breathe deeply or slowly, or otherwise control and shape your breathing in a way most human beings could never control their liver function, say, or production of red blood cells. Our bodies know to breathe in the way our hearts know to beat, but our minds can also know to breathe in the way we know to choose to eat chocolate ice cream, or in the way we know to run or dance. Breathing is quite literally both of the conscious mind and the silent knowledge of the body.

If walking reminds the mind that it exists only within a body, a body that has its own way of knowing things that reason cannot grasp, then breathing is the conduit between the body and mind. It is through breathing that the knowledge gained through the body and the knowledge and reason of the mind can begin to integrate, to teach each other. Walking physically pulls you out of the world of your mind, and can lead to the realization that you are deeply connected to a reality bigger than the one in your brain. Focusing on breathing quiets the constant noise in your head, the running commentary that distracts you from concentrating fully on what you are doing. When the mind is quiet and the body deeply connected with the surrounding world, something strange and unexpected and undeniably wonderful starts to happen.

Perhaps it isn't surprising that when I began to really notice my breath, I began to really notice God. In practices of many religious traditions, ranging from Buddhist mindfulness and Hindu yoga to Sufi *zikr,* breath is an integral part of prayer techniques, though in very different ways and with very different interpretations of what is going on. What they have in common is a focus on the breath as a way to somehow realize or approach a deeper understanding of reality.

After long days of walking and breathing, I began to notice something else seemed to be there, not in the air or in the ground, but everywhere—something quiet and not at all pushy, some presence that seemed to be a part of me and yet not just me. Through breathing, I began to become aware that something was with me, that I was connected to something, just as I became aware of that deep and silent connection between me and the old women in church through their breathing. Something big. The feeling made me want to look around and over my shoulder. Sometimes it came on gently, and sometimes with a bodily and mental jerk. It was not threatening, but it was not human. It wasn't déjà vu, and it wasn't an overactive imagination. It was just there, an often overpowering sense of hugeness, a vastness that was, somehow, oddly familiar. It was gentle, but there was also no mistaking that it was massively powerful. It seemed, well, friendly. And when I was aware of it, I could not remember how I had not noticed it before. I did not know what this thing was.

BECAUSE I GREW up Catholic, the best word I know to describe the presence I felt is "God." During the first few weeks on the Camino, I started to refer to God as "it" because the sense I had was of something like nothing I had known before, vast in scope and presence, and different from what I had always thought God to be. Whether or not I wanted to, and even though I had rejected it on an intellectual level, I had deeply absorbed the notion of God as an old man in the sky flinging lightning bolts at people, but what I came to sense while walking was nothing like the image embedded in my mind. Though I noticed this source of breath, this source of life, both in me and around me, something I felt as though I were swimming in, I did not dare approach or address this thing or being. That presence of life felt so close, but it did not correspond with what I knew about death, my father's death, and so I was afraid, very afraid.

13.

My father was upstairs in his bedroom getting ready to go to sleep for the night. He did not know anyone else was up there, so he left the bedroom door open as he prepared the dialysis machine and the bags full of dialysis fluid for the night. I was upstairs though, and I startled him as he stood half-naked in the alley created between the bed and the machinery, in a straight sightline from my bedroom door through his. He was hunched over, tethered to the machine by a thick rubber tube that stuck into his giant belly. It wasn't soft and jiggly like a fat man's belly, but firm like the red balls we used to play dodgeball in gym class, full of fluid and poisons that accumulated through the day. It looked tender and painful. His belly button was popped inside out like a woman in her last month of pregnancy. His belly button would eventually kill him. The pressure of all the dialysis fluid flushing in and out of his abdomen, gallons of it through the night and sitting in him during the day, caused a tear starting at his navel in the peritoneal membrane, the web of tissue that lines the abdominal cavity. The doctors did surgery to repair the rip, and during the time it healed, he underwent hemodialysis, where the blood is cycled through a machine and cleaned directly. The bacterial infection he died of entered his blood system during a session of hemodialysis. After three months fighting sepsis, strokes, constant diarrhea, sudden blindness, and a bleeding ulcer that required sixteen blood transfusions, he died on a Sunday afternoon in June. My mother, sister, and I were in the car, ten minutes too late. None of his family was there, but a nurse sat with him till he died.

His white underpants hung loose over the flat part where the cheeks of his rear end should have been, the leg holes gaping wide where his legs came out. His dentures were out and his face collapsed around his mouth. He swayed slightly on his black, gangrened feet with missing toes and half toes and flaking black flesh.

With one hand, he absentmindedly scratched at himself. He was always scratching, because his back and shoulders were covered with crusty white pustules caused by the failure of dialysis to screen out phosphorous the way kidneys do. The skin is the other excretory organ, and if the body cannot rid itself of waste through urine, the waste will erupt out through the skin. They itched him so badly that he scratched till he bled. All of his undershirts were stained with dried blood.

The machine was shrilly and incessantly beeping at him, and he could not figure out how to get it to stop. He held his head in one hand while the other rubbed his back. He sighed.

I didn't know whether to close my door or try to creep

downstairs without having to acknowledge him. I did not want that to be my father. I did not want to see him that way. I still do not want to see it, but I can see him standing there, defeated.

When I was a girl my father and I used to go for car rides early on Sunday mornings in his Austin-Healey. We flew down Sunrise Highway, one hundred and twenty miles an hour, with the top down, the wood floorboards of the car shaking, my whole body shaking, the wind in my face so I could not breathe. The car stalled and we had to get out and push, and then run and jump into the car as it rolled along. "Don't tell your mother," he said, the morning sun lighting up his curly hair and blue eyes. This was our adventure. Of course I would not tell.

There were other things I must not tell my mother: the cigarettes he smoked in the car, the dozen tiny hamburgers we would eat at White Castle, the chocolate ice cream I would scoop out for him in the kitchen after dinner while mom sat right there, thinking it was for me. These were dangerous, illicit things, and although they went against the family rules, and though I knew they were very, very bad for my father, I went along because I desperately wanted him to love me. While I adored him, he was not always kind to us, his children.

My father went into kidney failure the week before Christmas when I was a junior in college, but he had been diabetic since he was seventeen. I never knew him when he was not chronically ill, but everything changed once his kidneys stopped. His illness was no longer dangerous and something to be conquered. It became sad and shameful. My parents didn't tell anyone about dad's kidney failure for over a year. I told everyone at college, but I didn't want pity either. That began a long process of learning how not to feel, of trying not to feel.

PART 4

Anger

14.

On pilgrimage, the road itself is a microcosm of human life, shrunk down to five weeks or so. The first day, the twenty-some-odd miles over the Pyrenees, is birth. It's hard, but you end up in the beautiful Basque country, Navarra, lush and green, moist and soft, overflowing with roses and mud. That is life. But then you cross a ridge and enter the *meseta*, the Spanish equivalent of Nebraska, but with no Dairy Queens. It is about 110 degrees every day, flat, with few trees, covered in swaying wheat. There is no shade, no flowing water. You slug through this. The white straight chalky road stretches out in front of you, yellow wheat is all you can see on either side, blue sky with no clouds above, and the sun bakes and burns you. You cannot escape it. This is death. Then you reach another set of mountains. You climb over, and you descend into Galicia. It is even more beautiful than Navarra. Greener. Softer. With this really great white wine they serve in ceramic cups. You didn't think anything could be more beautiful than life; then you come here. And you appreciate it so much more, the green is so much greener, because you slugged through so much yellow brown wheat. The damp air is so much softer because your skin cracked in the dry sun. Your body is strong now; the blisters have become calluses and you can walk forever. You are so happy, so close to the end of the pilgrimage, but you never want this to end. This is the afterlife. Resurrection.

But first, you have to get through death.

• • •

ONE MORNING, AS the wheat fields were beginning but still interspersed with vineyards, Alex and I stood outside the doors of the *refugio* and slathered on sunscreen in the gray stone courtyard. The stones on the ground were uneven, placed in patterns of swirls and circles and diamonds framing ovals.

I dragged my feet all that morning getting ready for the day, but once outside, a sense of doom returned and I was desperate to start walking. I dreaded the sun and the realization that I would once again be in the heat. I was angry at myself for needing so much sleep, for not wanting to wake up, and for putting off the beginning of the day. The sun was already high in the sky at eight o'clock. I was panicking. I rubbed the sunscreen on as fast as possible.

Breath heaving, stomach in a knot, muscles tense, fingers clenched in a ball, I wanted to bolt. But Alex was still putting on sunscreen. Slowly. He seemed to be enjoying it.

"Aren't you done yet?"

"What?"

"Let's go. Come on. It's getting hot. Come on."

"I'm still putting on sunscreen. Give me a second."

"Let's go. You're taking forever. Come on."

Alex had gobs of sunscreen on his arms and legs, too much to be rubbed in all the way, and so his skin had a shiny white sheen to it. He squirted out a handful into his palm and proceeded to rub it into his face.

"Okay, I'm ready." He smiled at me.

He still had blobs of sunscreen on the sides of his ears and under his nose. This drove me crazy. I walked over to him and roughly rubbed it in. "Jeez, Alex." I turned around and walked quickly down the street.

The days always dawned cool and clear, but by ten the sun would really begin to heat up. By noon we were walking through wheat as far as the eye could see. From the top of any small rise you could spin in a circle and see only blocks of yellow or gold or pale green with faint zigzagging red lines running through them: fields of wheat planted at different times and the red-and-orange poppy flowers that floated above the grain, bobbing in the breeze like paper teacups. In the distance, on hills rising above the fields and with roads climbing out of the wheat to meet them, small towns huddled in on themselves. Always at least one church steeple rose from the town, sometimes high and graceful but usually short and worn down, the edges of the stone buffered to smooth curving shapes. The sky was the color of old blue glass bottles, with only whispy clouds low on the horizon. A giant blue platform for the sun.

The sun was everywhere. Everything seemed to have become sun—the wheat, the road, Alex, myself. I hated the sun. I hated the heat and I hated the relentless way it just kept beating down on me, regardless of how I felt or what I did. I hated the heat rash it gave me and the headache it caused, I hated how hot it was, but mostly I hated how inescapable it was. There was no shade anywhere, no trees, no buildings, and no clouds to blot it out, even for a few seconds. It burned right through the top of my head, like a skewer that ran down my spine and stuck me to the ground.

I did not want this sun anymore. I was in fear of the sun. I thought about it constantly. I began praying, both as I walked and at night before I fell asleep that there would be clouds the next day to block it, or some trees to throw shadows across the road. Day after day I begged as I walked. "Please please please God let there be some clouds. Or trees. Just five minutes of shade and it would all be okay. Please God. I'll do anything. Just some shade."

The sun kept shining that afternoon, as it had for the past week. I explained to God why I needed shade, or even better, a cool rain shower. No response. Anger welled up in my throat. Was it so much to ask for a single cloud? All around the waist-high wheat continued to rustle gently. I hated that wheat which never offered shade. I stormed three feet into the field.

Wheat hurts. It scrapes and burns. This just further enraged me.

"Fucking wheat. Goddamn fucking wheat."

A steady stream of expletives erupted from me. I don't really curse and it was a surprisingly liberating feeling. I kicked the wheat. It felt so good that I kicked again and again, circling around myself and kicking in every direction. With all my body weight behind me, I shifted onto one leg to let the other fly as hard and fast as I could. The backpack threw me off balance and I almost fell. "Goddamn backpack!" and I flung the thing off me. "Stupid sun! Couldn't there be any clouds! Nooooo! Of course not! All I fucking ask for is some fucking clouds, but never. I pray and pray for a cloud or a tree, but you just ignore me. You probably laugh at me. Goddamn fucking prayers are never answered. I am a good person, you know. Do you know that? Do you care? Do you fucking listen? All I wanted was a fucking tree!" I stood in a wheat field screaming at the clear blue sky and blazing sun. Silence. So I started kicking again and I didn't care that it hurt. It felt good.

"Why are you kicking the wheat?" Alex asked.

"Because it is not a fucking tree," I screamed back.

"Really?"

"Yes. And you should, too. Don't you hate it?" I asked, turning on him.

He rubbed the back of his neck and looked at me. "Why should I hate it? It's just wheat. It just stands there."

This enraged me even more. I started howling. I wasn't even using words anymore, but just sounds. I was shaking and screaming as loud as I could. I'd lost control of myself and I knew it. I couldn't stop. Was Alex such an idiot? Couldn't he see that the wheat just standing there was exactly the problem? That no matter what I did, I could do nothing to change the wheat into a tree? I was completely powerless. This was a betrayal of all I had ever been taught about hard work and responsibility and justice and fairness. I keep kicking.

I hear a click. Alex has taken a picture of me.

"What are you doing?"

"You'll want to remember this someday," he said, dropping the camera into his backpack.

I picked up my bag, stumbled out to the road, and started walking again. "I feel better," I said. Alex didn't answer.

We walked on in silence.

IF PRAYER IS the willingness to be open to and to accept the mysteriousness of God even if it doesn't fit into your neat definitions and ideas of how the world works and what God should be, if prayer is the attempt to understand God—and this is what I think prayer is—then losing it in the wheat field was the first time I had consciously prayed. Oh, I had talked to God before. That's what I did all day on the pilgrimage, since I'd learned that one is supposed to have an intention for the pilgrimage. I patiently explained to God that I needed to know what I should do with my life so that I would know which classes to sign up for in the fall. I wanted an answer so I would know that I could find a job when I graduated, something that would make me happy, because I certainly was not happy then. I figured God, if God existed, would know this and that if I asked nicely, God would tell me. I had no real interest in getting to know God. I just wanted information, not a relationship, not a relationship with such a weird, distant thing that had created a world where people died in gruesome ways, where bodies could malfunction in such disgusting and original ways. I had never thought of God as something I could have a relationship with, something I would want to understand, something I could feel emotion toward.

I could not even name the emotion that had been my general state of mind for years before that day. Everything infuriated me because I did not know what in particular angered me. I had no idea who or what I was angry at, or even that I was angry at first. I just knew that anger was all I seemed to be. It fueled me. And since the anger had no object, I was angry at everything around me.

It took me another year to figure out what I was angry about that day in the wheat. I wasn't just angry at the sun or the fact that my father had died. I was angry that the world did not function the way I thought it should, the way I'd always been told it did. I was angry that my father had suffered so much and that in the last years of his life he wasn't the man I knew as a girl. I was angry suffering and pain couldn't be avoided. I was angry at how powerless and out of control I was. I was so walloped off kilter by these things that I responded in rage and fear, totally moorless, but also totally open for the first time, no longer shielded by my own notions of what was true or real. For the first time I asked and truly wanted to know the answer: Did God even care? And what was this God that would set up such a world?

To be angry with God means to realize at the deepest level, a place that is both physical and emotional at the same time, that the world is broken and not as it should be. Anger at God is protest against suffering. That suffering can be caused by social inequity and structural injustice, but it is also caused by personal losses, physical pain, and the reality of death, our own and that of others—this cruelty built into the human condition. To be angry at God, not in theory or idea, but in the body—the anger that rises up from the solar plexus and out through the arms and legs and mouth—is to pray, for it is to lay bare, in the most intimate way, the wounds of life felt deep in the body itself, to expose them as though open to the sun, to expose the deepest part of the self to God, that unknowable Other who lurks in wheat fields on the sun-baked high plains of Spain.

15.

Some days I'd spot an olive tree orchard off in the distance as we walked, and say a prayer that the Camino would wind through the grove. The ancient, gnarled olive trees, no more than six feet high with small, sparse leaves, didn't give much shade across the Camino, but their twisting trunks were sometimes more than a foot across and I thought that I might be able to crawl right up under one of the trunks into its shadow. This day, as usual, the Camino went off on an unexpected bend, bypassing the trees and staying in the vineyards and wheat fields. This last part of the day we plodded through wheat turned rosy-orange by the slowly sinking sun. The air seemed to shimmer and everything had a golden glow, including Alex as he walked a few steps ahead of me. Though the Camino was wide enough to fit us both, we usually didn't walk side by side, even when we were getting along and singing songs together. We never decided do this, but by the end of the day one of us was walking eight or so feet ahead of the other and on the opposite side of the path. We stopped and waited for each other for water breaks or snacks, and always paused when there was a turn in the road. We even had conversations spread out like this, but it seemed that by the end of the day each of us needed the psychic solitude offered by a distance of eight feet, as though too much physical proximity would overwhelm whatever energy was left at the end of the day.

It was after four o'clock when we walked through a shallow valley closed in by dark, tree-covered hills on either side. There was no town in sight. The Camino stretched in a straight chalky line to the sun, which was now low enough to hit me square in the eyeballs under my itchy wool baseball cap. We had walked through the hottest part of the day, and it was a mistake.

Alex and I came upon a falling-down wooden shelter, turned both enchanting and sinister in the pink light. I don't know what the structure was—perhaps a farmer's shed. It was small and not as high as I am tall.

"I wouldn't go in there, Lumpy."

"Why not?"

"It's probably full of cow shit."

"It's full of shade, is what it is. I think we should stop here for the night." I didn't really want to stay there but I didn't want him telling me what to do.

"We are not stopping here for the night," he said. He was trying to sound like a father, I thought, firm and patient with a willful child.

"Why do you get to unilaterally decide where we stop for the night? I think this is a good place to stop. I'm sick of walking and there is no town anywhere near here."

"You want to stay in a shed full of shit for the night when it's still light out and we can still get to the next town. That is stupid. That's why I decide we are not staying here."

"It's not full of shit," I yelled as I crawled into the shed. "It's full of beer bottles."

Alex sighed in annoyance. "Oh, that makes it much more appealing. I'm walking."

"Fine. Go walk." I scrambled out and followed after him. This walking separately was not friendly. I was secretly happy we weren't staying there, because the shed smelled of urine and stale cheap beer. But I had no idea why I was feeling so ornery, why I wanted to pick fights with Alex, arguing for things I didn't even want, why I felt so angry when I wasn't really mad at him, why I fed off the anger and went out of my way to create situations where I could be angry.

Anger can be prayer, but it can also be destructive. When misplaced, it's dangerous. Anger that does not know what it is, anger that seeks to be felt and seeks to be understood by lashing out at the person walking with you—that anger is blinding. It blots out all signs of grace and life and love and unity and God. Anger that doesn't know what it is obscures everything so that you don't know where you are going. It takes a lot to break through the kind of anger that feeds on itself, never moving forward or back—stuck in one place, lost in the same spot. And, truth be told, that is where I was most of the time on the Camino.

I pulled out my book of maps. I love maps. I love being able to see where I am and where I'm going and, mostly, where I've been. I love maps because they give me a sense of place, but more important, they give me a sense of control. If I know where I was and where I am and where I will be in the future, I'll be able to control it all and prevent painful things from happening to me. Not only can I prevent myself from getting lost, but I can also protect myself psychically, or so my thinking tends to go. The maps we had of the Camino, though, sucked.

They were not the topographic maps you use for most hiking, maps that allow you to find your location using just a compass and your own eyes. These maps were hand-drawn in a way that suggested what the countryside might look like rather than an accurate diagram of it. So, for instance, if there were chestnut trees in the area, the map showed cheerful little puffy green treetops on sturdy brown trunks, but did not show that you climbed two thousand feet in less than a mile through those puffy trees. And because the maps were interested in giving an impression rather than an actual lay of the land, distances were approximations, with the scale changing drastically from page to page of the book. These were not very helpful maps.

Knowing all this, I clung to them anyway, unable to give up the possibility that I could find my way back into control.

"Let's see where we are on the map."

Alex, who usually humors me and my map love, who actually gets a kick out of it and asks me on hiking trips to name the mountains around us, turned around and said, "Why? It isn't going to get us there any faster. Why don't you just keep walking so you actually get to a town tonight." And he turned back on his heel and walked away.

We actually were quite close to the town of Los Arcos, perhaps less than a mile, hidden behind those trees on the bumper-like hills. We followed the signs to the *refugio* and had a wide-open view of it from about two hundred feet away. It looked like so many of the other modern municipal *refugios,* squat and surrounded by concrete and packed dirt. Dozens of people were sitting outside at picnic tables in front of it, laughing and talking loudly. A sign advertised a massage therapist available for aching backs and legs.

I didn't want to stay there with all those people and their foot rubs. I wanted to be alone and cry, but because I did not know I was sad (in the same way that I didn't know I was angry), this desire made no sense and so I didn't say anything to Alex. As we approached, a woman waved at us, a wide sweeping wave of her whole arm. It was Ines, the Australian woman we had met a day or two before, and whom we would run into the next day at an octagonal church.

She sat on a picnic bench with her wide sun hat squishing her curly hair. She offered us some dried figs.

"Careful you don't eat too many." She winked. "You two don't look so good."

"No, I guess we don't feel too good," I said.

"We think we're going to stay in a hotel tonight," Alex added. "Just to get a really good sleep." The quality of sleep available in a *refugio* was usually pretty poor. Inevitably, within a few minutes of the lights turning off, a wet and gurgling snore spread throughout the open dormitory, punctuated by squeaking bed-springs and the slam of bathroom doors. And every morning, starting at four-thirty or so—

"Bon jour!"

"Bon jour!"

"Bon jour!"

Frenchmen shouted to each other from across the room as they rustled their multiple plastic grocery bags. I'm not sure why so many pilgrims love to carry so many crinkling grocery bags, or why they need to shake them out and carefully roll them back up into little balls before dawn in *refugios,* or why they need to discuss how well they slept and their ingrown toenails from opposite sides of the room in the darkness, but this is the case.

"We saw a hotel in the town earlier today, didn't we?" The elderly but sinewy Australian rancher turned to his wife and Ines.

"But why don't you sit with us for a moment and rest before you walk over?" the wife with kind eyes asked. Alex and I shrugged off our backpacks and sat down, he next to the women and I next to the man.

"How are your feet?" he asked me intently.

I hope I learn how to do this someday—not just to rest but to allow others to rest, and to perceive in others when they need to be invited to sit down for a moment, when they need some-one to ask how their feet are, and be able to do so in a seamless, simple manner in which the receiver has no idea just how much she is receiving and just how much the giver is giving until much later, until years later when I read my diary and write these words and understand just what they gave me that afternoon, and I suspect what they gave to Alex. They gave us permission to rest for a little while not just from the physical work of the journey but also from the emotional and spiritual work. Maybe this is something you learn how to do when you become old.

I told him about my giant blisters that were healing nicely, and he told me about his achy joints and showed me his walking stick that helped take the pressure off. We talked about his ranch and the beach and the foods we like.

I glanced over at Alex every few minutes, to see how he was doing. The women were making him laugh. When he laughs, his whole face changes. He opens his mouth first into an "O" before the corners of his lips pull back into a smile, his eyebrows arch up, his eyes open wide and his head tilts back just a little bit, and for a second, before any laughter escapes him, he looks utterly surprised, as though continually amazed and delighted to find so much humor in the world.

THE HOTEL SAN MARCOS was rather nondescript from the outside, but the inside was decorated with posters of kittens caught in balls of yarn and colored glass bottles and figurines of shepherds accented with gold paint and more posters of kittens.

Our room, however, was much more austere. Alex threw his bag on one of the beds, and walked out onto the balcony. We still weren't talking, not out of anger now but from inertia in the stifling heat. I lay down on my back on the tile floor and tried to press as much of my skin into the cold ceramic as I could.

I wondered how long Alex and I would continue to not speak to each other. I worried that maybe we would never speak again, that maybe he would just take a bus to the closest airport, fly home, pack his belongings, and disappear from our apartment without leaving a note.

"Lumpy, hey Lumpy!" Alex often calls me Lumpy, a nickname from college that unfortunately stuck, and which he swears up and down has nothing to with my physical appearance. "Come out here. Hurry up!" He stuck his head in through the sliding glass door and grinned.

I scrambled up, sliding on the tiles, and outside to where he was waiting for me.

"Look!" He pointed into the sunset.

The ungainly form of a huge bird moved awkwardly across the sky like a thirteen-year-old running for the school bus. She flew over a basketball court below us where kids were laughing, pulled up short, and plopped down on an equally huge nest on top of a church steeple.

"What is that thing?"

"I think it's a stork."

As if in answer, the bird began to make loud and guttural clicking noises.

"Look, there's another nest on the other side of the steeple. And one over on the top of that building, too." Giant nests perched on the tops and edges of buildings made silhouettes against the red sky.

At dinner that night in the dining room of the Hotel San Marcos, we asked our waiter, an older gentleman, about them.

"Oh, the storks are everywhere. It's good luck for a town to have many storks, and for a house to have a stork. Good luck to see them, too. Bad luck for a stork to leave. I'm surprised—you haven't seen them before? Or heard them? Keep your eyes open and you'll see them all over. And now I have something for you." He smiled and clapped his hands together in anticipation before disappearing into the kitchen. In a moment, Elvis's "Heartbreak Hotel" thundered over the stereo system. He poked his head through the swinging door. "Do you like it?" he shouted.

At breakfast, he played Tom Jones for us.

ONCE WE KNEW to look for them, the storks were everywhere. On every church steeple, on the eaves of houses, and poles and platforms that I suspect were specially raised to encourage them to build a nest and stay for a while. If you couldn't see the storks, you could hear them from a distance, their insistent, odd clicking.

I grew up thinking of storks as big white birds dangling babies in blankets from their beaks, ready to drop an infant into some unsuspecting chimney and family, a euphemism for pregnancy and birth on greeting cards. In folklore stretching back to the Greeks, Egyptians, and Hebrews, storks were not the bearer of babies. Rather, they were the creatures in the animal world who taught humanity about filial piety. It was believed that a stork never left its parents, and cared for its mother and father into old age, even as it raised its own young and grew older itself. In medieval bestiaries, enormously popular illustrated books of beasts, the characteristics and behaviors of animals were interpreted to teach moral lessons. In these books, the stork was often depicted flying through the sky with her infirm and sick parent resting on her back. Did an artist or natural philosopher actually ever see such a sight in real life? Probably not, but that didn't matter. In books that described and discussed, in all seriousness, what could be learned from creatures such as the griffin, basilisk, unicorn, and antlion (the offspring of an ant and a lion of course), empirical evidence or even an eyewitness account didn't matter much. These were symbolic interpretations, not science as we think of it today. And in this understanding of the animal world, the stork was the paradigm of devotion and loyalty.

I wonder how a stork with a sick parent on her back would feel about that. I wonder if she would get angry.

Strange as this may sound, I think that part of my all-consuming anger was a misplaced attempt at devotion and filial piety. If I did not have my anger at dad, what did I have of him? What would be left? Now that he was gone I was afraid that all I could ever have of him was anger and regret. Since I did not want to lose him, I held on to that with both hands. Anger at myself, dad, Alex, the wheat and the sun and everything around me: that was my filial piety. I wanted to love my father because I had once adored him, but I really didn't know if I had any love or tenderness in me. I feared that if I lost the anger, there would be just a gaping hole where my father had once been. Anger was easier than sadness, easier than loss. It was easier to be angry.

I don't know where or when the storks started, but I suspect they were there long before I noticed them. Always there—loud and huge—and I just didn't notice them. It is amazing what you will not see when all you can see is anger. Not noticing was a theme just then: I did not notice the storks, and I did not notice God, and I did not notice Alex, as blind to his presence as I was to huge, noisy, swooping birds.

16.

Alex says that if you are going to spend the night alternately puking and shitting, the bathroom of a Parador, a Spanish luxury hotel sponsored by the government and often housed in a historic building like a castle or an old monastery, is one of the best places to do it. Parador bathrooms have cool and spotlessly clean white-tile floors to lie on, pleasant disinfectant-smelling toilets to grip, and cold marble walls to rest your sweaty cheek on.

The day he discovered this was a bad one from the start.

"DON'T YOU HATE how hot it is? I mean, don't you hate it? God, I hate it!"

"No, I don't hate it," Alex replied.

"How can you not hate it? You're covered in sweat. There is sweat dripping off the bottom of your shorts. How can you not hate this?"

"Because I ignore it. Just try not to think about it, Lumpy."

"What do you mean, just don't think about it? How can I not think about it? What was I thinking when I said I wanted to do this? Why am I doing this? This is so stupid."

"Just try to mosey through it. That's how we walk in Texas. Really slow, you know, just mosey. Don't let yourself be affected by the heat."

"Not affected by it? How can I not be affected by it? God, this sucks."

"Complaining is just going to make you hotter. Stop thinking about it, and you'll feel better."

"Oh, complaining about it makes me hotter? How would you know what would make me feel better? I feel better complaining. I don't just hold in my feelings like you, Alex. I express my feelings. I am in touch with my feelings and I express them. I don't try to deny how I'm feeling! And I feel hot!"

"You know what?" Alex stopped, and his soothing voice became sharp and aggressive. He squinted a little bit, stood up straight, pulled his shoulders back, and tilted his chin down at me. "I can't take this anymore. I just can't take it. I mean, what the hell is going on in your head? Why do you insist on making yourself as miserable as possible? I swear, I think you get off on your own misery! Is this some sort of fucked-up penance, or what?"

"Yes, it is! This is penance! I deserve this!" I wasn't sure where that came from, and I was immediately ashamed. "This is not a vacation! I told you that before we left! This is not a vacation!"

Like slicing open your finger on a razor-sharp kitchen knife, in that second when you understand exactly what has happened before the pain registers, I knew that I believed those words, and that I felt somehow calmed and comforted by the strife and misery I was creating on our pilgrimage.

Immediately I began to refute the thought. I just said that to upset Alex. I just said that for dramatic effect. I didn't believe in the notion of penance anyway. I wasn't buying into all that focus on what was wrong with me that penance seemed to imply. I was choosing to focus my life on what is joyful and life-affirming. Wasn't I feeling joyful right then?

• • •

WHEN MY MOM was a girl, she went to confession and penance every Saturday, like clockwork. She doesn't go anymore. Like most Catholics my age, I never went again after my first confession. A sea change has occurred in the American Catholic Church laity's mind about the sacrament of penance, often now called Reconciliation. Most people just don't go very much, but there's no single answer to explain why millions of Catholics' spiritual lives no longer included confessing their flaws to a priest and performing a penance.

For some Catholics, it's mistrust of the clergy, though the decline predates the recent sexual abuse scandals. It may be the growing acceptance of psychotherapy and medicine for treating problems like depression or anxiety. After all, it's been argued that one function of penance is to assuage guilt. Some trace the changes in Catholic's minds about confession to the Second Vatican Council and *Humanae Vitae,* when lay Catholics became aware for the first time that the furious debates that often surround theological issues, such as the morality of using artificial birth control, are not always so clear. Why confess to something when some experts disagree over whether it is even wrong?

My own reason was that I never understood the confessing part of it. Why did I have to talk to another human being to be forgiven by God? No one could ever answer that for me.

And since the confessing never made sense, neither did the penance. What was the point of saying three Our Fathers? It seemed like the spiritual equivalent of busy work and it made God seem petty and vindictive. Perhaps God wasn't so loving after all. His own son's atonement for humankind's sins was crucifixion. Such ideas can make God appear very brutal.

A common Catholic idea of suffering simply added to this

brutal image: the notion that suffering was good and holy because it could be merged with Christ's suffering and somehow save the world. But my father suffered greatly. I saw no goodness, glory, or salvation. Suffering and penance combined in my mind into petty demands of a nasty God.

THOUGH THE PRACTICE of penance stretches all the way back to the earliest of Christian groups in the first century of the common era, the forms it has taken and the meanings associated with it have changed dramatically in two thousand years. The earliest form, called "canonical penance" by scholars, was developed for reconciling a Christian who had sinned grievously with his church community. It was only done once in a person's lifetime. After publically confessing his sins to the entire congregation, he formally entered into the order of penitents, and even wore special clothing marking him as such, usually a hair shirt. For a matter of many months or even years, he lived an incredibly difficult and ascetic life, performing all sorts of trials, fasts, and vigils to prove his repentance. Once he was accepted back into full communion in the church and forgiven, also in a public ceremony, this time involving the laying on of hands, he would still, for the rest of his life, not be allowed to do many things, like serve in the military, transact business, get married, or if already married, have sex. Perhaps needless to say, early Christians avoided canonical penance or put it off as long as they could. They began to ask for it only when they thought they were dying. There was lots of debate among early Church fathers about whether penance should be allowed when a person was actively dying, for there could be no entering the formal order of penitents, no harsh fasts, no renunciations. Instead of reconciliation being granted after the penitential exercises were performed, it was granted immediately upon confession. If the idea of penance was that one needed to be reconciled with the community and needed to live out his life proving his desire and gratefulness at being received back into communion with other Christians, but could do an end run around this system by receiving penance just a few hours before death, what was the point? He wouldn't be rejoining any living community—he'd be dead soon. The idea began to develop that penance was not just for reconciling the Christian with his church, but that it somehow also reconciled him with God. This is a big development. It came to be understood that confessing one's sins and failings, asking for forgiveness, and fulfilling some sort of penitential acts would reconcile one with God.

In the sixth century, at the same time that canonical penance was being practiced in the Mediterranean, another form developed in Ireland. This form, based on short books of guidelines for confessors called Penitentials, also demanded austere penances such as fasting and sleeping on cold stone floors. For example, the *Roman Penitential* required someone confessing to homicide to do seven years of fasting, with three on just bread and water. However, there were some very important differences between celtic and canonical penance. First, celtic penance was not public as the canonical penance was. A person confessed only to a priest, not to the entire congregation. His penitential acts were done in private, and he was reconciled in private, again with only the priest. There were no lasting restrictions. And this form of penance was repeatable, as many times as necessary through a person's life.

The celtic and canonical penances shared something very important in common that differs from the practice of confession and penance as it developed in the medieval ages up through today:

Absolution was granted *after* the completion of penance. A historian of the practice of penance, Thomas Tentler offers the intriguing suggestion that early Christians found comfort in these forms of penance not despite the ascetic hardships but precisely because of them. They knew they were forgiven by God and Church, they knew they were cleansed and changed, because they were able and willing to go through such difficulties to prove it to themselves.

In the medieval period, penance took the shape of the celtic tradition of private penance, but absolution was granted at the time of the confession, not after the penitential exercises had been completed by the confessing sinner. Over time, the penances became increasingly light, even just symbolic. Three Our Fathers. Extra almsgiving on the next Sunday. These changes raised all sorts of questions. If not to change the heart of the penitent wanting to reenter the Church, what were the penitential excercises for? Was the priestly absolution releasing the sinner from the Church's required penance? Or was absolution somehow conveying the forgiveness of God? And if the latter, what, precisely, enabled a priest to channel God's forgiveness to the penitent? Was the most important element the sinner's contrition, as some theologians argued, or was it the sacramental power of the priest alone? And in that case, once again, what was the point of the ascetic practices of penance?

The shift to the idea that forgiveness comes through the priest's powers was not only a huge change from the early forms of penance, but also became one of the points that fueled the Reformation. Luther railed against that idea, arguing that justification comes from God alone, not through a priest.

The shape of penance as it is practiced today was set in the medieval era—the private meeting between priest and penitent, the necessity of regret, the asking of forgiveness, the absolution, and the assignment of a penance. The forgiveness was believed to come from God, through the sacramental power of the priest, and the penances were punishment due for the transgression. Why punishment would still be due for something already forgiven was never really clearly explained by anyone, but it set the stage for the development of all sorts of sticky theological ideas, like indulgences, and doing penance for other people (even dead people), and Purgatory, the place you go to after death to do all the penance that you didn't get to in life, before moving on to heaven.

SO IF I was so skeptical, why was some part of me doing the pilgrimage as penance? I knew that something was wrong, and maybe in my Catholic instincts and buried memories of the brightly colored Lives of the Saints books I read when I was seven, I found a possibility that had seemed to work for others. Maybe I thought making myself miserable would correct things.

I don't see it that way now. But the instinctual desire to do difficult and strenuous penitential exercises makes sense to me, even if confessing and absolution might not. When I was a little kid, I pulled my sister's hair regularly. She'd cry, I'd feel guilty, say I was sorry, and my mother and sister would forgive me. But then I'd turn around and do it again. I couldn't help myself.

I think penance is born from a similar set of circumstances. You might be really sorry about what you did to hurt another person or yourself, and God might forgive you, but this doesn't mean you won't turn right around and do it again. Sometimes destructive, hurtful patterns are so deeply ingrained that we continue to do them even when we don't want to anymore. We simply don't know how to change. Forgiveness comes from God, through grace, freely and lovingly. However, sometimes lasting change in one's behavior comes slowly and only through a radical shake-up in the pattern of one's life. A radical shake-up like walking on a pilgrimage across a foreign country.

I've actually found the notion of Purgatory helpful here. The root of the word suggests Purgatory is not punishment, but a state in which to purge, to purify, to cleanse, to make whole, to strip away that which does not belong. I have no idea if Purgatory as a place or time or state actually exists, but the idea of purging away that which causes sin—that which separates us from God and each other—helps me understand what penance could be.

Penance, however, also has a dark side to it, an element that is open to great abuse. There is a fine line between a deep desire to change and self-hatred, between penance and self-destruction, and I had crossed it somewhere in the rolling fields of northeastern Spain. I was, as Alex eloquently put it, getting off on my own misery.

"Well, I am not going to be a part of your self-flagellation. I'm walking alone."

He walked off ahead of me.

"Good!" I screamed after him. "This way I can express my feelings in peace!"

We walked apart for the rest of the afternoon, and did not wait for each other when the Camino turned or when we needed a drink. But neither of us let the other out of sight, as though some unspoken rule would not be broken, no matter how angry we were at each other. In the beginning, Alex walked ahead, and

I stayed forty feet behind him. I sent furious, fuming thoughts into his back.

After a while, though, my anger dissipated, because I wasn't really angry at him at all and I missed him as I watched him walk ahead of me. He moved his head left to right in slow turns, looking at the fields around him. He sometimes whistled, but never for more than half a minute. I wanted to know what he was thinking. I wanted to hear his funny comments and the silly songs he sang as he walked along.

When he stopped to look at birds' nests built up underneath a small sandstone cliff, I passed him. I was hoping he was waiting for me, but he didn't turn around as I approached, even though I made lots of noise and slowed down to give him plenty of time to notice.

As we neared the next town, Santo Domingo de la Calzada, I slowed enough that he caught up.

"The guidebook says there is a Parador in this town," I said.

We did not say another word to each other, but walked past both *refugios,* following the tourist signs through town to the Parador. This Parador was in an old pilgrim's hospital, founded in the thirteenth century by the namesake of the town, Santo Domingo, to care for sick and weary pilgrims.

We were sick and weary pilgrims, right? We weren't being bad pilgrims staying in a luxury hotel, right? We were needy pilgrims in a traditional pilgrim hospital, albeit one substantially gussied up. At the time, I didn't need to justify my behavior to myself, but later, as the black miasma of anger and depression first began to lift, I had a hard time understanding and accepting that I had once been so low and had acted the way I had toward others. I could not understand why my mind had ricocheted around from one extreme of emotion and conviction to another, from self-punishment to overindulgence, from treating Alex with cruelty to overbearing, saccharine kindness, from days filled with apathy to mania. It was as though the part of me that began to emerge from a cocoon, in its fragility, could not bear to look at the part of me that had been doing all the living that last year or so. I was embarrassed.

Only much later was I able to look back at that time with some gentleness and see a person doing the best she could, even if it wasn't very good. I was working as a chaplain a couple of years after the pilgrimage. I was sitting with a man who was dying of cancer. He'd told me the previous time I'd visited that he had been sexually molested by a priest when he was a teenager.

"You know what I realized this morning?" he asked in the dim light.

"No, what?"

"Everyone is doing the best they can, all the time."

"Yes," I agreed. We were silent for a moment. "Well, actually, sometimes, I could definitely do better."

"No!" He lifted his head from the pillow. "You see, that's what I mean! You think you could have done better, or should have. But for whatever reason, you couldn't. That was the best you could do. It might not have been very good—it might have been a failure—but if you could've done better, you would have. You see?" His head fell back onto the pillow, and light beads of sweat had emerged on his face from the exertion.

"What do you mean?" I wasn't sure that I understood the urgency in his voice.

"I mean it goes for everybody you meet. Even that priest. He was doing the best he could. And it wasn't good enough. It wasn't. But for whatever reason, that was the best he could do. I don't know why." He paused. "Once I realized that, it changed everything." He closed his eyes.

Staying in a luxury hotel, in a place far different from a *refugio* and away from the other pilgrims, was the best I could do—I'd reached a breaking point.

The lobby had high wood-beamed ceilings, red-tile floors, and soft lighting. It smelled really clean, that nice fresh clean smell, not the antiseptic clean of a hospital bathroom. Two bellboys promptly appeared at our sides and asked if they could help with our bags, and did not blink when we handed them sweaty, wet backpacks.

When we got to the room, I called the laundry service and asked them to wash everything. I didn't care that it cost me three dollars to clean a pair of socks. I wanted to smell like fabric softener for a little while.

We took naps and ate dinner at a convent, where plump nuns with shoulder-length veils they flipped behind them like flirtatious girls made trout and warm peaches, always making sure our water glasses were full. We fell asleep immediately after dinner, exhausted.

ALEX CRAWLED BACK into bed around five in the morning after his bout of sickness in the bathroom. He woke up for the second time that day in the late morning.

"Do you feel better?" I asked.

"Oh yeah, much better. I think it's all out of my system."

"Really? Do you want to keep walking today?" It was cool and misty outside, perfect weather for walking.

"Yeah, I do." He said it weakly. I didn't believe him.

He was swaying slightly as he stood there and a faint sheen of sweat had already appeared on his face from the exertion of standing.

"I don't know, Alex . . ."

"If you want to go today, I can go."

I really did want to go that day. This was the type of sunless day I'd been dreaming about. But it was clear that Alex shouldn't go anywhere.

"Why don't we just stay here another day? That way we can get to see more of the little town, and go to the top of the cathedral," I said. We'd seen people standing on the roof of the church, which was across the street from our hotel.

Alex spent the whole day in bed. I have no idea how he would have walked that day, and yet there is no doubt in my mind that he would have if I'd asked him to.

As I pulled the door shut behind me, he managed to croak from the pillows in which he had his face buried, "Did you lock the door?"

"Yes, Alex." I jiggled the doorknob from the outside so that he could hear that he was locked in safe and sound. Alex feels about locks the way I do about maps.

I went to the hotel spa.

ALEX SLEPT THROUGH the afternoon, but at six he sat up and groggily announced that he was hungry. As he searched the night table for his eyeglasses among the half dozen minibar ginger ale and Lemon Kas bottles, he decided he could not stand to be in that room anymore. We made it only as far as the lobby before Alex collapsed on an overstuffed leather sofa.

I went to the bar and ordered a round of sodas and five little appetizers from the long list of tapas in the leather-bound bar menu. Alex and I spread our linen napkins across our laps and sank into the sofa as a waiter arranged heavy silver knives and forks on the coffee table. We listened to soft music and the gurgling of the old fountain as we waited to be served our snacks on china plates and our sodas in crystal stemware.

This was not very pilgrimlike behavior—not at all. From the luxury hotel to the eighty dollars spent to have our laundry done to the hot tub to the gourmet tapas served as we lolled around on a leather couch in the lobby, the centerpiece of which was the original, rough-hewn well old Santo Domingo had dug to care for sick pilgrims. A trio of Irish girls who had spent more than one night on the Camino lost, sleeping in barns in the countryside, told us that if they did the Camino again, they would stay only in Paradors and bring "scads of money." Yet a few of the other pilgrims let us know, lifting their eyebrows and smirking when we met them in the street and told them we had stayed in a Parador instead of the *refugio*, that they did not think this was very pilgrimlike behavior.

There is an unwritten code of the "proper" way a pilgrim is to walk the Camino. It draws on modern notions of athleticism, competition, and toughness. In this code, the "real" pilgrims (and that is the term used) are those who start somewhere in France, carry their bags the whole way, never use any form of mechanical transport, stay only in *refugios,* and lose lots of weight. The less authentic pilgrims are those who have someone helping with the bags, stay in pensiones or hotels, or, worst of all, take cars or trains for part of the journey. Spiritual or religious motivation means nothing to those who want to classify "real" pilgrims from those they see as "cheating." In this hierarchy, the "real" pilgrims are those who suffer for the Camino. Those people who take a tour bus along the route, stopping at churches and shrines to say prayers and touch relics, most of whom seem to be religiously motivated but out-of-shape elderly folks, were not "pilgrims." They were—the most disparaging word of all in this view of the Camino—"tourists."

Though it is not clear how many of the modern pilgrims are aware of it, this modern notion of the pilgrimage as a test of endurance and physical sacrifice has a lot in common with ancient ideals of asceticism and penance.

Asceticism is a notoriously difficult phenomenon to define, but the action that most people mean when they use the term is that of renunciation of physical pleasures and dependencies. It can be a way to gather closer to God and other people by stripping away all that is unnecessary and blinding. Asceticism has been held up as an ideal throughout Christian history, especially while on pilgrimage.

However, when misunderstood and abused, it can also do just the opposite, and I think it is easy to misunderstand. It's easy to slide from asceticism to reveling in your misery, acting out a self-hatred, and then misunderstanding that this is, in fact, what you are doing.

The action of asceticism is renunciation, but that does not explain what asceticism does, why people engage in it, and what it is for. Some have argued that historically, asceticism functions as a challenge to the status quo, as a radical alternative to the way most people think life should be lived, to "reality." The early Christians' renunciation of sexual activity was a way to challenge and negate the importance of the family in Roman society, and thus challenge

Roman society and worldview in total. It was a way of proclaiming that a new creation was beginning.

But asceticism has never only been about social change. It's also about the transformation of the individual. In choosing to renounce all things, the ascetic becomes not deprived, but liberated from the fear of losing possessions, standing, or comfort. In choosing to deny oneself, the ascetic has nothing to lose and therefore is free to choose any path without the doubts and anxiety most of us must deal with when we make decisions, let alone radical choices. Paradoxically, in renouncing the things of the world, the ascetic is one who can embrace the world fully.

There were traditions of asceticism in both the Jewish and Greco-Roman contexts in which Christianity developed, and forms of renunciation can be traced back to the very beginnings of Christianity. But Christian asceticism really hit its stride when it started to become institutionalized through the practices of the earliest desert fathers, like Antony, ascetics who chose to live alone in the North African deserts, devoting their lives to prayer. It was these people who set the model for later Christian asceticism—celibacy, bodily mortification, silence, solitude.

Symeon Stylite lived on top of a pillar several different times in his life. He became quite famous and attracted throngs of the devout and curious. And so, in order to get away from the crowds, his pillar got taller each time. He spent four years on his first pillar, which was nine feet high; three years on his next pillar, an eighteen-footer. His third pillar was thirty-three feet high, and he did not come down from it for ten years. His last and final pillar-home, built by his followers for him, was sixty feet high (as tall as a six story building!) and only six feet wide. He lived, prayed, and preached from up there for twenty years. When, during this last time on a pillar, he developed gangrene in his foot, he chose not to come down. Instead, he observed and wrote about his dissolving flesh, amazed by the beauty and delicacy of his skeleton as it emerged through the rotting muscle. Asceticism allowed Symeon to recognize beauty in whatever shape it took.

Saint Catherine of Siena lived for months at a time eating only communion wafers. She also drank the pus from the wounds of those she was nursing back to health. But while Catherine's inability to eat was not something she herself chose or embraced, feeling that it was some sort of disease, her pus-drinking was something that she felt brought her closer to other people, and closer to God. Pus-drinking was about embracing all of humanity, even the gross parts. It was about love and communion. Both Catherine and Symeon's ascetic practices seem downright disgusting to my modern ears, but when you read Catherine herself talk about it, it takes on a different meaning.

Asceticism can be life- and creation-affirming, or it can be a disgusted rejection of the natural world and body. How one understands creation and the body determines how one approaches asceticism. If one sees creation as good and adequate, or even perfect, than the renunciation of asceticism is about freeing the body and mind from the materialism it clings to in fear, and embracing the simplicity and beauty of creation. If one sees the body as noxious, then asceticism is about denigrating the body because one sees it as hateful.

A friend of mine who became a nun when she was seventeen, almost fifty years ago, explained that the understanding behind reasons for celibacy have changed dramatically in her time in the sisterhood. At first, sexuality was seen as deeply tied to Original Sin, and therefore something to reject because it led one away from God. Now sexuality is seen as natural and good, and celibacy is seen as a sacrifice one is willing to make for the good of other people—a sacrifice that paradoxically frees one from the obligations of husband and children in order to serve all of humanity. The ascetic practice remains the same, but the understanding of why it is done has shifted to an embrace of creation through sacrifice rather than a rejection of creation.

THE DIFFICULTY OF walking in the sun and the asceticism that is a necessary part of the Camino—you just cannot carry that much on your back, and so your dependence on things necessarily is decreased—did play an important and positive role for me in beginning to deal with dad's death and illness. It did function as it should in stripping away all else and allowing the deep recesses of the mind to become louder, and in letting God become louder. I truly wish that I had been able to do the pilgrimage in the traditional, simple, ascetic way. But that's not what I was doing. I was pushing asceticism over the line, from a healthy stripping away of the extraneous into a destructive relishing of my own pain and suffering. That was hurting Alex, and it was selfish, as opposed to selfless.

What is the reason behind one's asceticism? If it is to punish oneself, it contradicts its own purpose, leading you deeper into self and away from God and others.

Asceticism, and the notions of penance that often go along with it, are very tricky and dangerous things. As with most powerful things, they can be put to a powerfully good use or a powerfully bad one.

Asceticism can wall you off from others, damaging or destroying relationships, as I learned. My insistence on a skewed asceticism while walking through the wheat, clinging proudly to my own misery, was draining and bludgeoning Alex. There is a place for being gentle with oneself, and a place to allow joy and humor. My skewed "asceticism" and "penance" were based on a skewed and very limited picture of God.

WE STOOD ON our balcony and watched the daylight fade into the misty fog. As darkness swallowed the spires of the cathedral, packs of teenagers wandered through the streets, singing at the tops of their lungs, the enthusiasm of each song building until it erupted into shouting and cheering. Alex and I listened to them, leaning over to see the groups of boys and the groups of girls as they walked and skipped and pushed each other below us. Their joy seemed almost tangible and I had to stop myself from reaching my hands down to them on the street below, wanting to touch their singing.

As anyone who has been angry for a long time knows, it is tiring to be furious. It is exhausting to be unhappy. That sour, punishing view of God and self and creation saps energy. But just across the way, in the cathedral, there was a correction of my view of God and this world in the form of two clucking, strutting chickens.

PART 5

Joy

17.

In a golden chicken coop set high into the thick walls of the cathedral of Santo Domingo de la Calzada live two white chickens. Alex and I called them the Holy Chickens.

People gathered below craned their necks up to see the birds strut around their small enclosure, ruffle their feathers, and peck at the ground. Whenever one of the chickens lurched up to the bars, a delighted murmur went over the crowd, and flashbulbs snapped in a flurry of light. Some people stood right below the coop, as close as possible to the chickens, and cocked their heads all the way back trying to see them. Some people stood against the far wall, leaning against the stones with their arms folded, quietly and intently appraising the chickens or waiting with cameras poised for the best shot, barely blinking. When a chicken spread its wings, as though about to take off in flight, a gasp of expectation and concern ran through the people below. When one of the chickens started crowing, the crowd applauded. People came running from other parts of the cathedral, eyes wide, mouths open, oohing and aahing, hoping to see the chickens in action. People lined up underneath to have their pictures taken. They were like rock stars.

Some people knew of the existence of the chickens before they came to the church, and made a beeline for them. But it was easy to spot those who didn't. When they stumbled upon this mess of adults looking up as expectantly as five-year-olds at the end of the Macy's Thanksgiving Day Parade pointing and squealing with delight, they followed the crowd's gaze up to the coop and then looked back to the crowd, up to the chickens again, around themselves in a circle and back up, blinking and straining their eyes. And then they laughed.

The chickens were the lead attraction of the cathedral. Yes, you could climb up to a balcony on the roof of the church and look out for miles over the rolling green and yellow countryside, see the sun setting through pink clouds spread across the horizon like cotton batting pulled apart, and little far-off towns like castles rising on gentle hills. The cathedral had its share of beautiful statues and reliquaries, and the great open expanse of still air under the arching, vaulted roof. But the chickens . . . how many cathedrals have their own two bright white chickens in a golden coop?

THE CHICKENS LIVE there to serve as a reminder of a miracle that took place in Santo Domingo de la Calzada many centuries ago, a reminder to all gathered underneath never to underestimate the power of the intercession of Saint James and his abiding concern and love for the pilgrims who journey on the Camino de Santiago. It is a story of illicit love, betrayal, loss, and even resurrection itself.

A young man named Hugonell traveled with his parents as pilgrims to Santiago de Compostela in the tenth century, stopping in Santo Domingo de la Calzada, perhaps staying in the pilgrim's hospital Domingo founded, perhaps even staying in the same room as Alex and me. The young man met a barmaid that night at dinner. He fell into a deep infatuation with the beautiful but duplicitous young girl. For reasons that are unclear to this day, she hid a pewter goblet from the tavern in the young man's bag, and then reported him to the authorities. When they searched his belongings and found the heavy cup, an item no poor pilgrim would carry all that distance, an item no poor pilgrim could afford, they immediately charged him with theft. He objected, pleaded for mercy, and protested that he had no idea how the cup got into his bag. But the evidence was against him. The magistrate sentenced him to death by hanging.

The next day, the sentence was carried out. Before his execution, the young man stood on the wooden platform, lifted his face to heaven, and called out to Saint James to help him, to vindicate him, to save him.

The trapdoor fell. The rope jerked. The devastated parents could not bear to remain in the town, and so continued on.

The parents traveled all the way to Santiago, praying for the soul of their beloved lost son. Once in the cathedral, they heard a voice. It told them that, miraculously, their son was not dead. He was still alive, hanging by his neck, saved through the miraculous intercession of Saint James. They must go before the mayor of Santo Domingo de la Calzada and rescue their son.

The parents rushed back. They burst in on the mayor as he ate dinner, crying that a miracle had taken place, that their son was still alive. A heavenly voice had told them so. The mayor, miffed at being bothered at his dinner table and incredulous at the impossible story the grief-stricken parents told, laughed at the mother and father.

"Your son is as alive as these two chickens on my plate!" he bellowed. "Now get out!"

But before the final words left his lips, the two crispy, roasted chickens leapt up on his plate and began to dance around the table crowing and squawking, knocking into bowls and bumping over pitchers.

The stunned mayor spluttered and waved his hands about as his obsequious servants chased the resurrected chickens, trying to control the damage.

"Enough!" the mayor bellowed again. "We must be off!"

The entire party ran to the gallows, where the young man still hung, waving in the breeze of a hot Spanish evening. When they cut him down, the young man was indeed alive (though suffering from terrible heat rash on the backs of his calves and thighs), and a great and joyous reunion followed. Much thanks was given to Saint James and the glory of God was proclaimed by all for this great miracle.

In the case of the Holy Chickens, it would have been enough to get a policeman to walk over to the body and poke it to realize the boy was still alive. Instead, two roasted chickens are raised from the dead to dance around and make a point. The miracle has been commemorated not by a painting or fresco of the saved young man, but by two living, crowing, squawking, pecking, strutting chickens.

THE HOLY CHICKENS made me very happy, almost irrationally happy. They seemed to make everyone happy. In the stores in town, a dozen different postcards with the images of the chickens could be found. Some were taken from a distance, with the entire chicken coop edifice on golden display, and some were close-ups of the chickens' faces in profile, like 1930's movie stars. I sent out a dozen postcards.

While walking the Camino, I just accepted that chickens would live in a cathedral. At that point, it seemed as reasonable as a woman who used an attack dog to alert her to pilgrims passing or the wine fountain in Irache. When I first read about the fountain, I envisioned red wine spilling over tiered marble basins, bubbling up like a geyser. It was actually more like a wine spigot, a tap sticking out of a wall of a winery with a large sign inviting all pilgrims to drink freely if they wanted the strength and vigor needed to reach Santiago. A much smaller sign off to the right warned pilgrims not to drink too much in the late afternoons, when they were probably thirstier than they realized, more dehydrated than they realized, and more likely to get sloshed than they realized. When we got there, a busload of German tourists, drunker than monkeys, were baking in the afternoon sun and wanting to take our pictures and hug us. Chickens in a church were par for the course at that point. But when I got back, all those people who received chicken postcards were baffled.

Why were there chickens in a church? they'd ask. I'd tell them the story of the miracle. Resurrected roasted chickens? they'd reply. And the guy hung by his neck, alive, for months and no one noticed? Why hadn't they cut the body down? And that still doesn't explain why there are chickens living in the church. Now if they had roasted chickens that could dance, that would make more sense, but they're just normal chickens living in the wall. Why don't they just have a painting of the guy hanging but still alive? Or a plaque explaining the story? And anyway, no part of the story took place in the cathedral, so why are the chickens there in the first place? The postcard receivers would look skeptically from me to the picture of the coop. Why are there chickens in a church? the skeptics demanded.

I was taught as a child, like thousands of others, I bet, that a church is "God's house." We expect things of the Divine to be in a church. In Catholic churches this is most explicit in the Eucharist. But there are other things in a church that one typically assumes should be in a church, and therefore things we assume should be markers of the presence of God and, somewhere deep in our minds, things we assume tell us what God is like. Sculpture or painting or mosaic or stained glass. Organ music. Candles. Bible. Holy Water. Solemnity. Seriousness. Power.

Chickens?

But there they were, upending whatever it is I thought of as a proper thing to see in a church, a proper thing to symbolize or signify or remind one of God. A marker that makes hundreds of people giggle and point, so that peals of laughter ring through the solemn, dim church, a marker that is joy. As my notion of what chickens are was ruffled, so, too, was my notion of what God is.

VICTOR AND EDITH TURNER, the preeminent pilgrimage anthropologists, and many of the people who studied pilgrimage after them, accepted the idea that religions divide the world into sacred and ordinary places. And perhaps this is accurate and that people do go on pilgrimage to go to a sacred place.

Or perhaps it is not so accurate at all, because I think the Camino was not just leading me to a sacred place, but rather, it was leading me to see the sacred in all its places.

In the iconography and texture of Catholicism in Spain, a world in which anything and everything can and probably ought to be seen as explicitly holy and sanctified, the chickens make sense. Everything can be a marker of God. Once this seeps into your psyche, everything does become a marker of God. The absurdity of visiting and watching two chickens in a gilded coop, hoping to hear them crow was like having blinders gently ripped off. On pilgrimage, I was learning to see the sign of God where before I would have only seen chickens. At some point, you either finally open your eyes to God, or you choose—and it is a choice—to keep them closed and not see. A lot of people I've talked to as a chaplain have certain expectations of God, and of how God *should* work in this world. In sticking to our static definitions of what God should be, I wonder how often we preclude certain aspects of what God is.

THAT NIGHT AS we walked after dinner, Alex and I passed an ice-cream shop and bought cones to eat as we wandered the stone streets. He grabbed my hand. When we passed another ice-cream shop, just a minute after I popped the last bit of leaking cookie cone into my mouth, he squeezed my hand and swung my arm up and down, and asked, "Want another one?"

I laughed, "Yeah, I do. Do you?"

"No, but I'll get you one."

Full of four scoops of ice cream, I leaned against him on a park bench in the town plaza under the dense awning of trees and watched the sky turn colors through the leaves and felt the cold ice cream melt in my belly and Alex's warm chest and arm on my back.

And yet, even after the chickens, I still wasn't able to recognize God's presence that night. The root of joy was still eluding me.

18.

I spent that night poring over the maps and pictures in the guidebooks, twisting my hair and peeling my lips, thinking of the wide blue sky and white sun.

When we woke up, the panic set in, and I raced around the room, stuffing things in my bag and yelling at Alex to get ready. He was already ready, of course, since he was always ready before me, having packed his bag and washed his face while I studied the unhelpful maps again and paced around the room. He sat quietly on the edge of the bed. We were supposed to start walking again that day.

I wanted to start moving again, but my stomach clenched at the thought not just of the open fields and the increasing June heat, but of what my mind would do, where it would go, and how I would respond to its rambling into places I did not want to remember, the exhaustion of many kinds that would follow.

The *meseta,* the high, wide, and hot, dry plains of Spain were approaching. I didn't want to walk across them. There was some remote corner of my mind that knew that while I was physically able to walk ten miles in searing heat, I might not be emotionally able to stand the fury in my mind. That corner of my brain sent out ominous warnings that would pop into consciousness at odd times, while eating an ice-cream cone, while bending over to tie a shoelace, while washing my face.

Alex watched me try to determine mileages and bite my lips as I packed. "I don't think I should walk today," he said, and looked at me straight in the eye when I stopped short and turned to face him. "I still don't feel right after that trout. I think it'd be okay to take a bus to Burgos today, since I'm still getting over being sick and all, don't you think?"

This took me by surprise. My mind slowed down, and the frantic speed, a feeling like a living thing, like a gnawing, running, scratching, digging hamster, drained out of me. Of course it would be all right to take the bus if Alex were sick. Now, if I were sick, that'd be different. The more punishment, the better. But for anyone else, it seemed the only logical thing.

The bus lurched around each corner on twisting roads to the city of Burgos. We saw a group of pilgrims once, where the Camino crossed the road, and I felt a pang of glee and guilt that we weren't also walking. We stayed for a few days in Burgos in a little pensione, saw the cathedral whose intricately cut stone spires look like lace, and the plain glass windows inside, a reminder of when Napoleon bombed the city and the reverberations shattered the original stained glass. We walked along the high wall of the old fortress on the edge of town, ran around in the fort, finding old cannons and playing hide and seek. And when my mind was not otherwise occupied, I thought about the *meseta*.

I read about the concrete sun shelters along the Camino that the government had built to offer pilgrims shade and shuddered. I read the guidebook's suggestion to stock up on several bottles of water in a particular town because there was no other water source for the next fifteen kilometers, and twisted my hair till I pulled it out. I read the average daily temperature chart and translated the numbers into Fahrenheit and then did the math again, picking at my lip. I showed Alex pictures of the wheat fields stretching as far as the horizon, and then described them out loud when he said he didn't want to look.

The night before we were supposed to start walking again, sitting outside of a little bar, eating *croquetas* and drinking sangria, Alex said, "Lumpy, I don't think we should walk through the *meseta*. I think it would be a mistake. I know this is not a vacation, but I think we need to take a vacation from the Camino."

"What?"

"I think we should skip the *meseta*. You're obsessed with it. It isn't normal."

"Alex, we can't skip it."

"Why not? Of course we can skip it."

I looked at him, unable to speak, heart beating.

"And I have to tell you," he continued, "and I hope you won't take this the wrong way, but I don't want to walk across the *meseta* with you."

"What do you mean?"

"I mean what are you doing this pilgrimage for? Is it to torture yourself? Is it to torture me? I don't really know, but somehow I don't think that's the point of this whole thing."

I looked at a stork circling overhead. She landed on a church spire. I waited a few seconds to make it seem like I was thinking it all through, but I wasn't. I'd made up my mind almost immediately.

"Okay."

"Okay?"

"Yeah, you're right. Let's skip it."

Alex shook his head. Now he was confused. He didn't know that this is what I had been hoping to hear, that this is what I wanted, but that I needed someone to give me permission to take a rest, and that it would be all right.

THE HOUR-LONG train ride to León sped us over the treeless land we would have spent five days walking. Getting off the train, I experienced my happiest moment yet on the pilgrimage: I saw a Pizza Hut. I was on vacation.

• • •

LET ME EXPLAIN about Pizza Hut. I grew up on Long Island, New York—a place populated by hundreds if not thousands of small family-owned pizza parlors with names like Phil's, Gigi's, and Carmela's. Places that make pizza eighteen inches across, thin and delicate-crusted with light, piquant tomato sauce, sweet creamy mozzarella cheese, and a little sprinkle of basil on top, eaten with each slice folded in half lengthwise so it could be held with one hand and the sauce and cheese and sausage and meatball and whatever else was on it wouldn't slide out or off. When we went to pick up the pizza every Friday night when we were little, we watched the pizza guys twirl lumps of dough into wide, thin circles that draped over their fists. If they weren't too busy, they'd tossed one into the air for us.

I first ate a slice of Domino's pizza when I was a freshman in college in rural Virginia. My hallmates ordered a "bacon cheeseburger pizza." It was the most terrible pizza I had ever eaten, but it was the only thing available to eat at one in the morning besides the peanut butter crackers from the vending machine in the laundry room. I ate it, but I didn't think of it as pizza. It was more like an interesting regional specialty.

The only time I had eaten in a Pizza Hut before León was while visiting Alex in Texas when he was in law school. We went with one of his friends to a Pizza Hut buffet lunch. I felt vaguely ill afterward.

But once in Spain, once I saw that red glowing Pizza Hut sign in the train station in León, my feelings changed. The Pizza Hut, with its neon signs and Pepsi refrigerator, its offerings of regular or family-size pizzas, had the only food my body wanted to eat. I longed for Pizza Hut, for the bland dough, for the canned tomato sauce taste, for the thick and oily cheese. I longed for the way the oil from the cheese is absorbed by the crust at the place where you fold your slice in two, the way that cheese oil, turned orangey-red by the tomato sauce, seeps into the dough turning it into a luminescent, pale orange, flaky sculpture, delicate and shimmering. I longed for the deep contentment in my belly that quickly turns into a solid rock. I longed for home, for my family and friends, for the familiar, symbolized by a small Pizza Hut in the León train station.

Alex and I found a hotel (we didn't even bother to look for the *refugio*—we weren't pilgrims, after all; we were on vacation!), dropped off our belongings, and headed back out. (No need to shower—we weren't sweaty. We had ridden in an air-conditioned train!) We walked right back to the station and ate a family-size pizza.

I forgot about the wheat and sun and anger and the growing sense of regret and guilt. I forgot about how much I wanted to get out of my own skin, eating hot oily slices of pizza till we stumbled out of the station and down the streets crowded with other strollers in the coming night.

For the next two days, we went to the municipal pool and spent hours lying on the grass in the sun I had hated just days before, playing tag in the water, and complimenting each other on how we looked in the mandatory cheap gray plastic swim caps we had bought at the pool's concession stand. Each night we returned to Pizza Hut for another family-size pizza and cans of Pepsi.

On the third day we saw the frescoes of Saint Isidore, remarkable thirteenth-century frescoes covering all the low, arched ceilings of the burial vaults, but spent the afternoon siesta at the pool, followed, again, by Pizza Hut.

If the greatness of a vacation is judged in terms of tranquillity, or forgetting what you were doing before, or the deep restfulness, then the Pizza Hut in the train station and the municipal pool of León may be among the greatest vacation destinations on earth.

Like finding your old baby doll—mine was named Bethany—in a trunk in your mother's attic when you were only looking for a pair of gloves, the same feeling came over me at dinner that second night in the train station—the feeling of most unexpected, almost forgotten, pure joy that enrobes you from the outside and wells up in you from the inside. The thick barrier that walled me off from my own feelings came down a bit and love for Alex and for pizza and for the sunshine surged up and over it and made a run for it while it could. The joy couldn't be contained. But now that it was loose, I started feeling again.

IF CHICKENS IN a church can be a reminder of God, a Pizza Hut in a train station can be, too. To enjoy pizza and Pepsi, to laugh with Alex for the first time in a long time—this was to allow a chink in the protective armor of self-hatred—a chink that would allow me to acknowledge this God I could not seem to get away from. In blocking my emotions, I'd also been blocking a relationship with God. Joy made a space for God.

A FEW WEEKS later we met the three Irish girls again in the monastery at Samos, where we had taken a detour to hear the monks chanting. We were in Galicia, the final green, mountainous, and remote stage of the pilgrimage. The day had begun misty and cool, and ended soft and shady in a town next to a mossy stream, under the wide canopy of old trees. We all sat outside at the local bar that night, drinking cold and fruity red wine and eating *caldo gallego,* a soup of potatoes, cabbage, and white beans.

The Irish girls talked about how the greenness of the mountains after the *meseta* seemed almost like a hallucination—it was so beautiful, so ripe and alive, and they never thought they could ever feel such strong joy about the color green before, feel such happiness at walking under arching and shady old trees. I would never be as drunk on the color green as they were.

But that was not an inebriation for me to experience that summer. I got Pizza Hut and a swimming pool, and a reacquaintance with the softness of happiness.

PART 6

Listening

19.

When walking becomes what you do, all that you do, when that meditation becomes a natural part of the rhythm of your day, you become very good at listening. I listened to my feet hit the ground, to my hands brushing alongside my shorts, to my breathing, to my heart beating, to the fluid whirring in my ears, and to the wheat rustling in a breeze I could not feel. I got very good at listening to what goes on inside me and outside me, very good at listening to sounds and words in my head and in my body. After awhile, you begin to realize that not all thoughts necessarily sound like your own, that there are subtle, fleeting emotions that usually get overlooked, and longings and desires you didn't even know you had. You begin to see that many events in your life are not as random as they first appear. You begin to suspect and then to be sure, when you listen intently for so long, that something you did not notice before exists in you, in your mind, in your heart.

I REMEMBERED ONE morning in León, in those last few minutes before fully waking up, when you are neither asleep nor awake, that it was Father's Day. It was a comforting thought at first, but once my eyes opened, it was as if the three previous happy days had weakened my ability to stamp out memories, and they shot out in my mind like soda that has been shaken and bursts out of the slightest opening in a can.

My father knew something was wrong with his mind well before his wife and children did. What I thought was cruelty and selfishness was psychosis. A neighbor who had suffered and survived a brain aneurysm was given some water from the spring at Lourdes, which she shared with my father. She was Jewish, but willing to try anything that might help.

Dad and I stood together admiring the plastic bottle shaped like a trecento Madonna, with an oversized white crown as the screw-on bottle cap.

"I know everyone thinks I need this for my body, but I don't. I need it here." He tapped his head with the bottle, and stared at me intently. "Something's wrong here."

He was waiting for me to say something, wanting something from me, but what he was suggesting both frightened and eluded me. I didn't ask him what he meant.

"Dad, you've been a nut for much longer than some magic water can undo."

"Ha-ha!" he cackled in the fake laugh that he had those last few years. "Yeah, I guess that's so. Who knows for how much longer?" He reached out his hand, and put his palm on my cheek and smiled at me. As thin as he had become, his hands still felt the same as they always had—like soft leather covering thick padding. His hands never became bony, even at the very end.

The tenderness of the gesture was too much. I walked away.

ON A CLEAR fall day with light chop on the water we drove down to the marina where we used to keep a boat. We sat on a bench just inside the gate, because he couldn't walk very far.

"Do you believe in reincarnation?" he asked.

"I don't really know."

"I do. I just don't think that this can be it. And I hope I do come back. I hope things will be different. I worked as hard as I could and I think I deserve to come back with things better." He stared hard, not at me or at the water, but at the scrubby grass in the middle distance.

"How would you want things to be different, Dad?" I expected him to say that he wanted to be healthy, that he wanted to live a long life in a body that did not betray him. That he didn't want to live in pain.

"I want to be rich."

I turned and looked at him. "What! What! You are in like the richest five percent of humanity! You are rich! Wouldn't you want to be healthy?"

He looked surprised. "I never thought of that." He paused. "I want to be rich so I wouldn't have to worry about your mother."

I think he forgot what it felt like to be well. I don't think he even considered it a possibility, as though he was always fated to be sick, as though that was a part of his character, a part of his being. But I didn't understand that then, so I shook my head and rolled my eyes.

I LIVED IN Austin with Alex during his last semester of law school. It was after college, and I was living back at my parents' house. I'd only gone out to visit him for two weeks over his spring break, but when it was time for me to return to New York, I just didn't go to the airport. I didn't want to return to the sadness and the tension, I did not want to return to a place where food was the enemy, and where the phosphorous levels of potatoes and cheese caused arguments that could be heard down the street, and the air of anger and fear lingered for the rest of the night.

"When are you coming home?" my younger sister demanded

on the phone. "This is not fair for you just to leave like this. You just can't leave."

And then, a few months later, another phone call from my sister. "You have to come home now, Kerry. Dad has gone crazy. You have to come home."

Dad had tried to hit my seventeen-year-old brother with a shovel. Because dad was so weak, he was unable to heft the shovel higher than knee level. When my brother jumped out of the way, my father barraged him with insults. My older brother was home that day. He pushed my father by the shoulders up against the door of the shed to stop him and shook him, demanding to know what the hell was wrong with him. My father began crying and then my brothers did, too. My sister called me.

I kicked a hole in Alex's wall. My sister was right. In the dynamics that are peculiar to each family, I was the bitch. I was the fighter. I felt I needed to go home and fight.

ONCE HOME, MY father gave me a card. He had signed everybody's name, but I knew it was from him because it was in his handwriting. He had probably found it in the jumble of cards my mother had bought but forgot to send and that ended up piled in a desk drawer. A little puffy house with round puffs of smoke rising from the pink chimney was nestled between two puffy hills, below a rainbow stretched through the sky. The message "I Miss You" was written across the bottom. Inside, dad had written, "We all missed you."

I tossed it to the side. He didn't know I had come to do battle with him, that I had come to defend.

• • •

MY FATHER'S RAGES were daily. Some were new and unexpected tirades, but most were repetitions of the same delusions and confusion. For example, every few days, dad accused us of stealing twenty dollars from his dresser drawer. We all knew that this twenty-dollar bill didn't exist, but in surreal fashion the dinner table erupted regularly as though we were reading from a script. My mother would quietly urge us to give the money back if in fact someone had taken it this time. At first, we pleaded with my father, but quickly we all started screaming. The food became cold, the mashed potatoes hard congealed lumps. We all became very skinny.

WE HAD A gray lop-eared rabbit named Ivan. This rabbit followed people around the house and would jump into your lap whenever you sat down.

One day dad kicked Ivan in her side (yes, Ivan was a girl—it's very difficult to tell the sex of a baby rabbit) and sent her skidding eight feet across the floor.

"Hey! What are you doing?"

"None of your business."

"You just kicked the rabbit. I just saw you kick the rabbit across the room."

"It's none of your fucking business."

"It is, too, my business. You can't kick the rabbit. What is wrong with you?"

"Don't you fucking yell at me!"

"I will too fucking yell at you when you don't even act like a human being!"

He shuffled off, veins bulging in his temple in anger. My fists were clenched. Ivan hid under the couch.

• • •

IT WASN'T ALWAYS that way. When I was thirteen, the age at which all my friends began to experiment with alcohol and cigarettes, my father found empty wine cooler bottles in the garbage. He said nothing at the time, but a few weeks later, when we were at a neighbor's party at a restaurant, my father brought me over to the bar.

I stood there awkwardly.

"C'mon, sit down." He motioned to a stool. I sat gingerly, looking to see where my mother was. "If you're going to drink, you should drink the good stuff."

I didn't know my father knew that I had been drinking. I braced myself to be yelled at, as I knew my mother would do, or to be told that I wasn't allowed to go to my friends' houses anymore. But instead he turned to the bartender and ordered two glasses of Johnny Walker Red, straight and neat. He put one in front of me.

"Cheers!" he said as he lifted his glass. I sat there, terrified and confused. "Now you lift your glass and say 'cheers.' "

"I don't know, Dad. Don't you think Mom will be mad?" In fact, I was desperately hoping Mom would come and save me, because this stuff made my nose burn just smelling it. What could it possibly taste like? This was no strawberry Bartles & James wine cooler.

"No, not at all. Take a sip."

It tasted like lighter fluid. I shuddered against all my will. "Umm, I don't think I like this stuff, Dad."

"You have to sip it slowly. That's how adults drink it. This is what people who know what's good drink, not wine coolers. You do want to drink what adults drink, don't you?"

Here was the dilemma, which my father hit upon so perfectly. Of course I wanted to drink what adults drank. I wanted to be an adult. That's why we had wine coolers. (And that fact that they made us tipsy.) But now that I knew that this was what adults drank, I was stuck.

My father made me sit there and drink the entire glass with him (which certainly could not have been good for a brittle diabetic, but I imagine he told himself it was for the good of his daughter, and not his own enjoyment).

I don't know if my father really thought Johnny Walker Red straight and neat was "the good stuff." I suspect he just thought it would be something very unpleasant for a thirteen-year-old. I never got to ask him. But I did stay away from hard liquor until I was in college, much longer than my other friends who had curfews and punishments and breath tests when they came home at night.

FOR MY THIRD birthday party my parents made me a Raggedy Ann cake. I know that was the occasion only because my mother tells me this. What I remember is Raggedy Ann's boots made with shiny black icing. I wanted so badly to touch those boots, to touch the liquidy smooth color, to see what it was made of. But I couldn't, because I was hiding under the table. People kept bending down and putting their faces near mine, or suddenly thrusting their hands toward me, trying to pull me out, scolding me for hiding. They told me I couldn't have any of the cake unless I came out, but they didn't understand that I could not move. I so wanted to see the boots, but I was frozen. I started to cry. My father crouched down, and put his head under the table. I touched his hair. He said I could hide as long as I wanted, and I could come out whenever I wanted, and then he handed me a piece of cake topped with black icing and let me eat it all by myself.

THE LAST TIME I danced with my father was at a cousin's wedding. It was fall of my first year in div school and he would be dead that June. We were separate but facing each other as we danced to some Motown song from the sixties. He moved jerkily and awkwardly, shuffling his feet and grinning. He grabbed my hands and tried to pull me in to him to dance as a couple, but I pulled away and stayed three feet away. I wonder if some part of me knew it would be the last time, knew that he wouldn't dance with me at my wedding, and so I could not get too close.

LYING ON THE hotel bed with my legs dangling over the side, I was crying and shouting, trying to explain to Alex what a terrible person I was. He stood against the wall not agreeing with me. If Alex only understood what I had done, he would be disgusted with me. So I yelled at him to help him see how terrible I was. He sighed heavily and rested the side of his head against the wall.

I shouted, "You just don't know how bad I am. What kind of person treats her father that way?"

"Lumpy—"

I cut him off. "I have never been so sorry for anything in my life." Immediately I heard, clearly and distinctly, a voice that was not Alex. It said, "Stop this."

I knew exactly what "this" was: the clinging to self-hatred. On a very deep level that I knew but could not often admit to myself, I liked the self-hatred. I was proud of it and I was comforted by it. I couldn't be such a terrible person if I could at least see how terrible I was. The self-hatred was a way to try to redress the wrong I felt I had done. It was something I did not think I could give up, for the fear that if I did there would be nothing left of the twenty-four years I had known him—nothing left of me.

Just as the voice said to stop, and before I could think, I felt intensely warm, different from the heat of the sun or a hot shower. I knew that I was forgiven, that I always had been, and I knew that I must stop. And I did. Somehow, it just lifted up from me, off of me, and out of me.

I walked around the rest of the day expecting the feeling of forgiveness to leave me, expecting to sink down into the place where I knew that I was completely unlovable—by God, humanity, or myself. Alex and I sat outside in the square in front of the cathedral at a little café and drank bottles of Lemon Kas, and I waited and waited for the feeling of forgiveness to leave, but to this day, it hasn't.

My own acceptance of myself in the last years of dad's life was much harder and longer in coming. But the knowledge of forgiveness, both God's and my father's, never waned.

I told a friend about hearing this voice, and she believed me. She asked, "Was it very gentle and loving?"

Well, no. Not at all. It was not mean or angry, but it was not necessarily gentle or soothing. It just was. It said, "Stop this." Not only could I, but I had to, because it was real. I had no choice. What I thought was impossible and what I thought would destroy me was the easiest thing I have ever done. I stopped not just because it was possible, but because it was the only thing possible.

So now I listen.

PART 7

Beauty

20.

The next day, our last in León, I finally went into the cathedral we had walked by and sat outside of for days. The stained-glass windows in this building are some of the most extensive in Europe, stretching almost from floor to ceiling, interspersed with just the thinnest columns of masonry, as though the glass were the supporting walls and the stone the decoration.

The afternoon sun lit up the flowers and vines and patchwork geometric shapes. The colored light pouring down through the nave landed on the people milling about.

It isn't known for sure when people first started to make stained glass, but one of the oldest fragments found is from the seventh century. Around 1100, a monk named Theophilus wrote down how to make stained glass, the first recorded mention of it. By then, the medieval technology and artistry of creating colored light through glass had been perfected. The colors don't actually come from pigments in the glass. They result when different minerals and metallic oxides are added to the molten sand or silica. These elements act as filters, blocking out some of the spectrum of natural light as it passes through the window, letting only some of the colors of light through. Gold makes reds, copper makes greens, and cobalt makes blues. Because it isn't dyed, stained glass does not fade.

The earliest stained-glass pieces tended to be more abstract, the artists using both the colored blocks and the black lead casings that held them together to create stylized images or patterns of light. In the fifteenth century, the glass artists shifted to trying to create realistic representations of people and events and stories. The lead was no longer a part of the design but rather something to try to hide and minimize.

I'd always been taught that the stained-glass windows in churches were there to teach illiterate peasants Bible stories. Most of the windows in León did not depict things, let alone scenes from the Bible in enough detail that a person could know what was going on. And much of the windows were too high to make out anything at all, except for the beams of gold, purple, and crimson filtering down through the dust. The point of these windows was beauty, not education. I walked in slow circles around the church, stopping in the crossing to see the colors fall on the church in four directions, varying in intensity and depth depending on how much sunlight struck the windows. The windows were so high that vertigo set in when I strained my head up to see to the tops, the shapes swirling and turning and dancing as the ground spun under me. It felt as if the light were pinning me down in transparent color, but at the same time, I also felt that if I just stretched enough, I could touch the tops of the hundred-foot-high windows. It was like having the bed spin after a night of drinking too much, except that I was in a church, and it was beautiful. It felt like there was nothing else I should be doing in the world except looking at those windows.

The twelfth-century Abbot Suger of the Abbey Church of Saint Denis believed that beautiful things lifted the soul to God. The twentieth-century theologian Hans Urs van Balthasar thought that God could not be known unless we recognize Beauty, and that Beauty makes Truth good, and Goodness true.

Beauty and a sense of beauty (and by this he does not mean simply a pretty appearance, but a transcendental truth) is the key to understanding the Glory of God, which is Love.

I TOOK A picture of the wheat fields the day Alex took a picture of me kicking them. I wanted proof of how horrible the landscape had been.

Everyone who looked at our pictures paused at that one. The stalks shine in the sunlight and sway to the left on a soft breeze. The braided tops of the wheat in the foreground are defined and distinct, intricately shadowed in brown and gold relief. As the eye trails away to the horizon, the wheat becomes gentle gradations of color, yellow to gold to beige to brown. The sky arches above, the blue apex the perfect opposite of the yellow. Low, white wispy clouds hover. The whole photograph seems to move.

"This is beautiful!" people exclaimed when they saw it. I thought they were crazy just after we got back, but now I, too, see that the wheat is beautiful. Perhaps one has to be ready to see beauty just as perhaps one has to be willing to sense God.

21.

Because the church was made from the same stone as the outcropping it huddled against, it looked as though it were an ornate growth on the sheer and rough cliff. The church was built into and out of the cliff, both surrounding and at the same time emanating from a cave where a small statue of Mary had been found.

The statue, according to legend, was found in 1052 A.D. by King García while out hunting. His falcon found her lodged in a limestone crevice.

In the eleventh and twelfth centuries in Spain, the religious importance of images, like this statue, soared. For the first thousand or so years of Christian history, devotion to saints was directed at relics, which tended to be in churches. And since Mary is believed, first in popular lore, then in official Roman Catholic doctrine, to have been assumed bodily and whole into heaven at the end of her life, there are very few relics of Mary—some of her clothing, a few drops of her breast milk. (Why Mary thought to save any breast milk is just one of many mysteries surrounding her.) But with the rise in western Europe of the notion of images as markers and even sources of the sacred in this world, little shrines to Mary exploded out into the countryside, statues here, paintings there. Throughout Spain, statues of Mary were found in caves or in fields. A shepherd out wandering found her image in a crevice, or a farmer would dig her up. Story after story tells that upon finding a statue, the people in the nearest town would try to move it into a church or a private home. Somehow the statue would escape and be found the next day, stubbornly in the place where it was first unearthed. Mary, apparently, wanted to be in the countryside.

Relics were in church buildings, but Mary was out in the places where people lived and worked. An image of Mary could transform any space into a sacred place. She belonged to the people, to the poor and the illiterate, as well as to the elite who could afford to buy relics and the clergy who controlled churches.

• • •

BEFORE ONE GETS to Mary in the cave, one first walks down a narrow stone staircase into the crypt below the church, and passes through the Pantheon of Kings. Row after row of marble sarcophagi of kings and queens of the twelfth and thirteenth centuries stare up at you, tiny people no more than five feet tall, smiling women and stern men, some with the muted remnants of their original bright paint still visible. It's sometimes hard to remember, looking at the cold white and gray stone statues in Gothic cathedrals, that they were once as colorful as the stained glass, that sometimes even the stone columns and pillars were painted in colorful stripes, that the inside of those cathedrals were not meant to be cold, but to be a riot of color. The kings' and queens' stone faces have been worn down with time, softened and smoothed by the touch of the living. The air was stuffy and dense—underground air shared by too many people. At the back of the Pantheon is the dark opening leading to the cave where the statue was found.

SOME OF THE Mary statues that popped up in caves are black with oxidation and are known as black madonnas. Some people have argued that the black madonnas are throwbacks to a pre-Christian, earth-mother goddess. Or, it's possible that the images were hidden underground during the Muslim invasion of Spain in the seventh and eighth centuries. Or maybe Mary, for some indecipherable reason all her own, wanted statues of herself in caves. Hard to say.

As interesting as the cave-dwelling madonnas are, perhaps the most famous encounters with Mary in this world are apparitions. Apparitions are different from visions. A vision is understood to be in the mind of the seer. While an apparition might only be seen by one or a few special people, it is understood to have a reality other than the one in the mind; it is believed that Mary *really* did appear in this world, and not just in the mind's eye.

Apparitions of Mary almost never happen in a church. Like the statues, they occur out in a field or in a grotto somewhere, and not to the elite and educated, and not to clergy. No, she always appears to someone poor and powerless, usually uneducated shepherdesses or farmers, like Bernadette or Juan Diego. A priest can say I have the education, and the training and the ordination, but when a person says the Virgin Mary herself appeared to me, well that trumps education any day in terms of who gets the power. Scholars often point this out—that the poor and women can gain religious power by having an apparition. But it often feels as though these scholars are saying that it is the poor who choose apparition as an avenue for power, and not that it might be Mary herself who has chosen to appear to the powerless and the poor in order to subvert the institutional structures of power. Maybe Mary likes to surprise and challenge the way things are. Maybe she's not meek or mild at all. Maybe she's a loose cannon.

A GUARD LETS in only two or three people at a time, because the cave is so small. The air in there is completely different from the air in the crypt. It is cold and wet and heavy with the dark smell of earth clashing with the cloying sweet smell of lilies. The statue stands on a table all the way in the back, toward the left. It's similar to other madonnas we had seen. A vase of drooping white and pink Asiatic lilies stands next to her. The table is lit by a bright spotlight, but the bare cave walls are left dark and undisturbed. It's cozy in here, despite the chill and smell and the harsh shadows, much more comfortable than the splendor of the Pantheon of Kings. Like entering a womb.

STATUES OF MARY used to show up in caves, and then apparitions used to appear in meadows and forests, and now images of her show up on the sides of mirrored high-rise buildings. Now you get Mary everywhere; she is uncontainable. She shows up on tortilla chips, in tree trunks. People see her all over. I have no idea if Mary really chose to show up on a potato, but I do know what it tells me about the human desire to see Mary everywhere. The hope of what Mary symbolizes, the possibility of human beings to carry and give birth to the divine in this world, to be creative in the sense of creating with God, explodes out into everyday life. This happens not in places of power but everywhere. It throws open where we can do God's work, where we can turn toward God. And if she is showing up on tortilla chips and bank buildings during rush hour, she has a killer sense of humor.

But there is a danger here. Confusion can happen when people begin to separate the symbol from what it symbolizes, when people begin to ascribe magical powers to the statue itself and forget that the statue is a representation of something larger, something intangible. This sometimes happens with statues of Mary, and with lots of other images as well. Mistaking what we humans can see and grasp for the transcendent, which by its very definition is just out of reach—ineffable—is the risk of trying to better understand the Divine with a human brain. It's this danger that has led in the past to bouts of iconoclasm, of destroying images in an attempt to refocus people's attentions on the transcendent. But there's a problem there, too. If the transcendent is, by defintion, above human understanding, how in the world is a human being supposed to get any idea of what this Thing is like? So you might end up banishing the danger of idolatry but find yourself left with no way at all of understanding how or what God is.

I'll stick with the statues. With the stained glass and the music and metaphoric poetry. I'll risk reading God too much into the beauty around me rather than risk missing where God is trying to get my attention through the avenues I can understand.

PART 8

Love

22.

We staggered into Villafranca del Bierzo in the late afternoon. We'd once again made the mistake of passing by a town in the early afternoon when we were still feeling energetic, and instead actually chose to push on in the boiling heat of the afternoon until we were on the verge of hallucination. You would think Alex and I would have learned not to do this, but no, we never did.

When we got to the *refugio* a harried woman asked us to wait a moment, then walked out. This *refugio* had a special mention in the English guidebook, which said it was completely financed and run by a family who had dedicated their entire lives to the pilgrimage. The father was known as a healer, and if you were lucky, said the book, you might get to be part of a special ceremony involving some sort of flaming drink and lots of storytelling. Alex was thrilled by the idea, having a lifelong love of flaming foods, drinks, and objects.

We went outside to peek around. The *refugio* was not a single building with bunk beds dormitory style, as most are. Instead, this *refugio* was a series of dirty green platform tents connected by muddy paths. It was like a beehive, with pilgrims swarming in and between and all around the tents. Youth groups prowled the compound in packs.

We waited a half hour, but the woman didn't return. Bruno, a man we'd met a few days earlier, walked over to chat. Then another pilgrim walked over, too, with her camera. She asked what tent we were in.

"Actually, we're waiting for the woman in charge to come back," Alex said.

"You know, there's another *refugio* in this town that just opened up. If I had known about it, I definitely would have stayed there," Rachel said. "It's really beautiful. It's in an old monastery."

Beautiful sounded good.

When we got to the Monasterio de San Nicolás, a long, high staircase lead to double doors dwarfed by the huge stone facade of the building. Inside, pale green and purple light filtered through the stained-glass windows and hit the white marble floors and pastel frescoes on the walls. The air was cool and gentle and the silence deep, like lying under four wool blankets in the dead of winter. It was more beautiful than the Parador.

The building had been a monastery and college for Jesuit priests, the young man behind the counter told us. Long lines of clean white beds in the former students' dormitory served as a *refugio.* But they also had private rooms. With full baths, and a view.

We took the private room. We went to dinner in the restaurant housed in the monastery's courtyard. We sat next to a gurgling fountain while the setting sun sent long, sharp shadows against the far walls, watching geraniums turn from blinding red to soft dusky burgundy in the encroaching shadows, eating veal and asparagus and chocolate cake.

I FEARED BEING a failure at the Camino. We weren't acting like all the other pilgrims, who stayed in *refugios,* ate egg sandwiches, and plugged on day after day. We "rested" every third day, rode in an air-conditioned train across the *meseta,* and stayed in more hotels than pilgrim hostels. We were actually gaining weight on the trip. I wanted to do this pilgrimage right, and do it better than everyone else. In the past, this was what had earned my father's approval, and I thought his love as well. I was lovable because I was successful.

I wanted God's approval, this likable if unexpected thing I had noticed while walking and breathing. I wanted to earn God's approval, and failing at a pilgrimage seemed just the thing to disappoint God.

I'd always been told that God loves us, that God is love, that God so loved the world, and on and on, blah, blah, blah. I knew that Christianity teaches God loves unconditionally. But it is one thing to know it and another to believe it or feel it. Yet all along, walking with me, as obvious as the nose on one's face, was someone who was teaching me what unconditional love looks like. Alex definitely could not have loved me for what I was doing on the Camino. He loved me despite what I was doing, despite how I was acting.

The signs were there, they were all there, but I didn't see them. It wasn't until we got home, and much time had passed, that I was able to remember and understand what was going on.

ON THE FIRST day on the Camino, back in Saint Jean, I had felt like a jackrabbit—nervous excitement propelled me forward with a speed and endurance that my body doesn't really have, except when hopped up on adrenaline.

Our hostess, Maria, woke us at five and hurried us down to eat, shouting that it was a long walk that day and we needed as much daylight as possible. She hurried us again out the door into the chilly and dark morning. The caffeine and carbohydrates, needed to counteract my addiction to Tylenol PM, made me twitch. I bolted out the door and up the Pyrenees.

The land was very, very green, and the road was very steep, but the steepness got my lungs and heart going and my legs striding. I walked fast, past the boulders strewn in the short and thick grass, past the ten-foot-high iron cross encircled by a wrought-iron fence in a pasture, past the old chestnut trees with giant trunks and peeling bark and dense shade, and up the smooth pavement road, not stopping to look around, not stopping to take a drink, not stopping to snap pictures. I just kept going, propelled by fear and coffee.

Until we came to a little stream where two women were soaking their feet. We stopped to soak ours, too, and when I pulled off my first boot I knew what I had done. I peeled off my sock to reveal a giant, oozing, popped blister. The women, both nurses, winced, and encouraged me to take a look at the other. Too late, I felt the hot spot—in fact, the screeching burning went all down the back of my other heel. There was a blister there, too, but I didn't feel it till I saw the other.

For the first of many times, a stranger bathed and cleaned my heels. But convinced that if I slowed for a moment I would end up in the dark, alone, cold, hungry and surrounded by wolves, afraid that I could not really do this, I pushed on full speed anyway.

The nervous energy carried me over three peaks, but at the base of the fourth, it evaporated, replaced by plain dread. A few miles from Roncesvalles, the monastery where we would stop for the night, the pain from my heels stopped me cold.

Alex suggested I wear my sandals with the canvas straps tucked under my heel. I made it only about three hundred feet before it became obvious I wouldn't make it very far. My feet kept sliding sideways and rolling, or a sandal would flop off.

"I don't know what to do. I can't keep going like this," I wailed.

"Okay, give me your backpack."

"Why? What are you going to do with it?"

"Just give it to me."

"What are you going to do with it?"

"I'm going to carry it up the hill for you."

"You can't do that."

"Stop pissing me off. Give me your bag."

He slung my red backpack on himself backwards, leaning it on his chest, a counterbalance to his own backpack, which he carried the correct way.

"Okay, I'm just going to go straight to the top, so if you need to stop, just catch up with me. I don't want to stop once I get going."

Without another word, he was off, and walked quickly and steadily a couple of miles up the last uphill of the day.

When we got to the summit, I said, "Thank you, Alex."

"Yeah, well, remember this the next time you want to yell at me about not putting my socks in the wash."

I was thankful, and awed, and realized that this was the act of a very generous person, but I didn't get it. I didn't understand why he had carried my backpack, and why he was so gruff about it, why he had brushed off thanks as though it embarrassed him. I didn't understand this was his way of saying I love you. I didn't recognize love as love.

23.

In a small town on the end of the *meseta* after León but before the mountains separating the plains from Galicia, an ATM machine ate Alex's bank card. It would not give him any cash, but neither would it give him a receipt explaining what was going on, or most upsetting, his card. The screen simply flashed an error warning and then went blank.

"Huh. Lumpy, you'll have to go in there and tell them their machine ate my card."

"Why do I have to go in there?"

"Because you're a girl, and people always pay more attention to girls. And you're much more charming than me. People always like you better."

"I don't want to go in there. Besides, it's your card and your account so you have to talk to them."

"I don't speak Spanish. Come on Lumpy . . ." Alex started wheedling.

"Uggh. Fine."

When I approached the teller, hunched over a ledger printout, he said there was nothing he could do to help me. I went back outside into the bank lobby, where Alex waited in front of the machine, and told him the bad news.

"That's ridiculous. We need the card if we want to eat for the rest of the trip. It's not like it fell down a volcano. They just have to open the machine and get it. Go back in there and ask to speak to the manager."

Why couldn't Alex just do this himself? Why do I always have to be the one to deal with strangers? Why do I always have to be the one to pay the pizza delivery guy or tell the cabbie where to go? Why do I have to be the one to talk to the bank manager? But I went in and asked to speak with him. He politely listened to the problem, and then said he was too busy to do anything about it, and shooed me away with the back of his hand, as though wiping crumbs from a table. He went back to his reading.

Back in the lobby, I told Alex.

"What's he doing?"

"Umm, it looked like he was reading."

"Oh, but he can't come out here for thirty seconds and give me back my card, a card that his machine swallowed with no provocation or reason? Tell him we're not leaving till I get my damned card."

I sighed and walked back into the bank. Before I could even get the manager's attention, though, a ruckus erupted from the lobby. Alex was bludgeoning the ATM machine with his fists.

"What! What is going on?" The manager jumped from his desk and, with clenched fists and arms straight down by his sides, strode out. I followed.

"What are you doing? What is he doing?" The manager yelled at me and pointed at Alex as if Alex was my dog.

"Alex, what are you doing?" I asked.

Alex started kicking the machine with his heavy boots like an unruly but determined toddler. "I'm getting my card," he said.

"He's trying to get his card," I reported to the manager.

"Tell him to stop this!" the manager said, jabbing his finger at Alex so I would relay the message as quickly as possible.

"Alex, stop this!" I said to Alex.

"Not till I get my card. Tell him I'll stop when I get my card. Gimme my card!" Alex kicked and smacked the console even harder. I could see by the tightly repressed smile breaking out in the corners of his lips that he was enjoying this completely. All of the tellers stood up to watch him, apparently afraid a robbery was in progress.

"He just wants his card back," I said to the manager.

The manager started yelling at Alex in Spanish. Alex started yelling back in English. As far as I could tell, their entire conversation consisted mostly of curse words, but they seemed to understand each other. I backed away and stood in the doorway between the bank and the lobby. Everyone inside was now staring and pointing at me, though I wasn't doing anything. I smiled meekly.

After a final flurry of yelling and banging, the manager threw up his hands, pulled a key from his pocket, and handed Alex his ATM card. It took him less than five seconds. Then the manager stormed back into the bank, shooting me a dirty look as he passed.

"Alex, I can't believe you did that," I said, waving at the people in the bank as if this would somehow calm everyone down.

Alex was wearing the little smirk he gets when he is particularly pleased with himself. He said, "I was just getting their attention. I knew they'd pay attention to us if they thought we would cost them money." I stared at him. He kept talking, sort of a corollary to my calming wave. "That's basically what I did all day as a lawyer, only on paper. This worked out great for everybody. I got my card back, and it was much faster than the manager thought it would be. And now he can go back to his romance novel without you pestering him. See how handy a law degree is? Who are you waving at?"

"Nobody," I dropped my hand.

"Besides," he said, obviously convinced of his own ingenuity. "Wouldn't you have freaked if we didn't have my ATM card for the rest of the trip? That would have meant that whatever was in your bank account would have had to cover both of us. I wouldn't have worried, really, but I thought you would."

"That's true."

"So I figured the worst that could happen would be getting arrested. I wouldn't mind. It would be worth it to keep you from worrying. And it was actually kinda fun." He waved good-bye to everyone in the bank still staring at him, and then stepped out the door and back onto the Camino, humming "C. C. Ryder" to himself.

I waved again and followed after him.

I MET ALEX when I was nineteen years old, sitting on a bench in front of the university's library on an October afternoon. He says he walked over because leaves were falling around me and he didn't want to read any more Emily Dickinson. Apparently, during a high school literature competition in Houston, he had learned that all of her poems could be sung to the tune of "The Yellow Rose of Texas." That day, he couldn't get the song out of his head, and I looked like an interesting distraction. After we talked for a while, I saw him later that afternoon as I was walking home. Alex was coming up the street as I walked down it. I waved. He waved back, and then started running, full speed, directly at me, up the hill. When faced with a boy I barely knew hurtling toward me, looking like he was ready to tackle, the only response I could think of was to run back at him. About five feet away, I jumped, and we collided. After we picked up all the notebooks that had gone flying, he looked at me and said, "Hmmph. I can't believe you did that. Most girls wouldn't do that." I learned later that doing something strange was some sort of informal test to make sure whatever girl he was interested in would be fun to date. I was the only person this ever worked on.

Do I look for the possibility of humor in God because Alex makes me laugh? Is this because I recognize God's love in Alex's love? Probably. Maybe this is why Holy Chickens mean something to me while another person might just be ironically amused. Perhaps this is why some of the other signs and symbols of God in Christianity are not meaningful to me. Perhaps each person has to discern for herself how to understand God in a world that has spent millennia coming up with ways to understanding and grasping that which is always ultimately beyond human reach.

PART 9

Community

24.

I took a picture of my shadow as we left the town of Rabanal del Camino, because I wanted to have a picture of myself that morning. I planned on being a very different person by the end of the day. I didn't know how to tell Alex this, and so I snapped my shadow against the scrub and gravel and guardrail as we walked. We were on our way to the Cruz de Ferro.

We had heard about it only the day before from Rachel, the English girl who was something of a celebrity while we were on the Camino because she walked in a short cotton skirt and a brown string bikini top, with her long red hair piled high in a bun on the top of her head. She used to sunbathe outside the *refugios* when everyone else was washing out their socks and popping their blisters. She was the undisputed Babe of the Camino.

The night before, Rachel told us about the tradition of laying down a stone at the Cruz de Ferro. It's a small iron cross on top of a thirty-foot-tall wooden pole, a marker for travelers in bad weather and fog. At the base of the pole, a giant pile of stones spreads out like a Christmas tree skirt. Ideally, you're supposed to take a stone with you from home and carry it all the way to the Cruz de Ferro, where you climb the twenty-foot pile of rock and place your stone at the base of the pole. The rock you carry is not just supposed to represent your burdens, or be a symbol of the heaviness you carry around with you. When every few ounces of weight feels like five pounds after a few hours in the sun, that rock literally *becomes* your burden, physical and emotional, which you lug around for several hundred miles before giving it up and laying it down on the pile. According to Rachel, you just need to tell your rock everything, spill your guts to the stone. You have to be honest with your rock—no keeping secrets from it or yourself. Then, when you put the rock down, your burden and the heaviness you have been carrying will be laid down with it, because your sadness has seeped into the rock with your words.

This sounded great to me. It was just what I needed—I wanted to lay down my anger. I was ready to put down my grief. I just couldn't believe I hadn't heard about this before.

I didn't have a rock, though. I sat in the back garden of the *refugio* after washing out my clothes and hanging them on the clothesline to dry. The line stretched all the way across the length of the walled-in patch of grass and sagged with the weight of dozens of wet socks and T-shirts and baseball caps. Rachel lay stretched out on a towel like a cat in the sun and a group of pilgrims kicked a Hacky Sack around. As the sun dipped below the stone wall, I made a plan. I'd pick up a rock first thing in the morning and then focus all my energy and force into the rock in one concentrated dose. I thought through exactly what I needed to tell the stone in as few words as possible.

I had a lot of time to make up with my rock and a lot to tell it. I was determined that everything would seep into it so I could put it all down.

On the way out of town the next morning, I bent down, pretended to tie my shoelaces, and scooped up a jagged gray, palm-size stone. I hung back behind Alex so he couldn't hear me, and I told the rock about my father, about my anger at him for being sick, and my anger at the way his behavior affected my sister and brothers and mother. I told the rock about how disgusted I was at myself about the way I acted and the way I was feeling. I didn't tell my rock that I was sad, because I was not aware I was sad at the time, and I did not tell the rock I missed my father, for it would be another year before I realized how much I loved him, and another six months after that to realize I missed him. Standing in the shower in my apartment in Somerville, two and a half years after he died, I was trying to figure out what to do because I was being sexually harassed by a Buddhist monk at my school field education placement. Should I confront the monk? Tell my boss? Would anyone believe me? I was lathering up the shampoo in my hair, trying to think of middle-aged white men I could talk to about it. Should I ask the school's fielded director? A professor? What middle-aged white man should I turn to? Then I realized: I wanted my father. I wanted him so much that waves of emptiness convulsed through me. I missed him. I missed the way he gave advice. I missed the way he would lay his hand over mine when we talked about something important. I missed the way he smelled. I had not missed him for two and a half years, and when I finally realized it, I felt as if something was being wrenched out of my chest through my mouth. I sat down on the edge of the tub and I cried. I had been missing him for years, since even before he died, and didn't know it.

But on the morning I walked to the Cruz de Ferro, I told the rock about anger. That, I thought, was the extent of whatever grief may be. If I could put down the anger, I would be done, and I would be a normal person again. As I walked I kept up a steady babble, and I clenched the rock hard. I squeezed it harder and harder as I climbed, determined that if I could not tell the rock all I needed to, I could press my anger and self-loathing into the jagged, cold lump.

• • •

IT WAS A beautiful walk that day, cool and cloudy. It felt like rain. The Camino climbed slowly and gently through rocky land covered with low brush and sweet-smelling yellow flowers. We passed through an abandoned town where the buildings were slowly crumbling into piles, but a freshly painted mailbox still stood, and an almost abandoned town, where one family lived in a tidy and neat little house surrounded by ruins.

We rounded a corner, came up over a steep little ridge, clambered over a guardrail to walk along the paved auto road, and there was the Cruz de Ferro. I thought I would see it from a distance, like a beacon. I thought it would be bigger. I didn't think it would be on the highway, but I didn't care. I could barely manage shallow breaths as I walked over to the gray stone pile against the gray sky. I was ready. I was determined. I was focused on my rock and my feelings and I was going to end this grief thing. Had I not been told that it was time to stop? And didn't I already feel better, lighter? Wasn't I honest with my rock? I was ready to be the person I was before my father died. I was ready to finish grieving and move on in life.

But that isn't how grief worked for me. Some people argue that it isn't how it works for anyone. The popular idea that grief has a distinct end, a set cycle in which you can track your progress, is not what I have experienced. Grief is more chaotic than that. You go back and forth between emotions, and your connection with the dead person does not end. Grief changes, but it remains, and the pain can return at any time—your graduation, your wedding rehearsal, the first time an appliance in your first house breaks, and you don't know how to fix it—the missing will continue because your bond with the person continues.

On one hand, this is appealing, this idea that your connection with your dead loved one can continue, that you don't need to give it up. On the other hand, there is a certain relief in the idea that you can be done, you can get over it and continue on as you did before, with the dead person nicely repositioned in your life, like a picture on the mantel to look on fondly at Thanksgiving. I liked this latter idea that morning. I wanted to be done with being tired and angry and empty. I wanted to leave it all in Spain on a rock pile.

I stood at the bottom with Alex while we waited for a man to walk down to the ground. He wiped his eyes, smiled at us for a second, and climbed back on his bicycle. "*Allez!*" he yelled and was off.

I squeezed my rock and chanted "anger and guilt" over and over like a mantra so that even if I forgot to tell my rock something, those two words would cover it all. I slowly climbed the pile repeating my phrase. The rocks crunched and slipped a little bit. As I got closer, I began to discern what all the bits of color I spotted at the bottom were. I was amazed at all the things on this pile. Once I got to the top, there was stuff to look at everywhere.

On the pole, people had tied bunches of wildflowers picked from the surrounding fields. Notes, some encased in plastic sandwich bags and some open to the rain and sun, with ink streaming down in dried rivulets, were stapled to the pole. Where in the world did they get staplers? Did they carry them all this way just to staple a note to the pole? Painted rocks, some with messages or words or names, some painted with pictures and designs, were strewn along the base. People must have painted their rocks at home and brought them all this way. Photographs, old pictures from the fifties and sixties printed on small pieces of paper with white borders, and more modern pictures, school portraits and snapshots of people with their arms around each other, lay tucked under the rocks to hold them down in the wind. A huge black marble plaque with the name of a ship inscribed in gold lettering leaned against the bottom of the pole. Who in the world lugged that huge, heavy thing all this way? I could barely make out the Spanish words on one note, "Please help me get to Santiago. My feet are so sore." How bad must his feet have been if that's what he used his one wish on? Another note had a poem in German and a pen-and-ink picture. Who was that a portrait of? Was he dead now, or just waiting back at home in Germany? Or was it a portrait of the artist himself? Who put all these rocks here? There were so many of them. How many pilgrims must have passed by here to create such a huge pile? Most of the rocks were pretty small, and I had noticed that down at the bottom of the pile the rocks were even smaller and sandy. How long ago did the people who left the rocks that are now at the bottom of the pile pass by here? How long did it take to ground them down to sand like that? How long would it take till my rock got smashed down to dust or fell to the bottom of the pile? What burdens did other people put down when they put down their rocks? Which rock had the man who came before us put down?

A dog nudged my left hand with his nose. I looked down at him, and he let out a soft whine. Another dog came up behind him and leaned against my right leg. Their skeletons showed clearly and starkly through their skin, and they averted their eyes from me. Very gentle, and neither of them barked. Did they live here, like guardians of the rock pile? They pawed the ground and sniffed my outstretched hands. I had most of an accidentally purchased dried-tongue sandwich in my backpack. There was no way I was ever going to finish it. I thought about giving it to them, but then decided not to. I was scared they might follow us or become aggressive. I still regret that decision.

I slowly walked down the pile. Almost at the very bottom, I realized I had missed it. I missed my moment. My moment to be free of grief. I didn't even remember putting down my rock, let alone feeling a sense of freedom or of a burden lifting because I had been too interested in all the other people who had put down rocks and pictures and notes. Nothing happened when I put down my rock. My mouth fell open.

I was not free of grief when I walked down from the top of the Cruz de Ferro. I was just at the beginning stages of it. That day, however, I did understand that I was intimately connected to all these other people who came before me and whom I did not know and never would know. I knew that their stories, their pain and their struggles, had supported me, quite literally, as I carried my rock up to the top of the pole by walking on the pile made by what they tried to leave behind.

The Cruz de Ferro, that pole topped by a simple iron cross stretching to heaven, grounded in a massive pile of stone, is a symbol of what the Church should be, of what I experienced the Church can be, while I was a pilgrim. The relationship with God may be deeply personal and intimate, but it becomes possible in the context of the people, struggling together, supporting one another together on the way. I could not have been a pilgrim without the support of all the people I met along the way, named and unnamed, and I could not have learned how to begin to recognize the quiet whisperings of God all around me if I hadn't been a pilgrim that summer.

When I think of that pile, all those stories, all that heaviness to lay down at God's feet, this life seems like too much for any person to do. The feeling I came away with from the Cruz de Ferro was not that I handed over my heaviness to God, but rather that I could bear it. Life, by the very fact that it ends, is set up to cause grief. Anger and sadness and loss can't be avoided. The heaviness of grief is like blood—it's built into our bodies, gushing from time to time through wounds that remind us of how vulnerable we are. We can bear the weight only when we do not bear it alone.

25.

Alex and I ate magdalenas, orange and honey sponge cakes with crunchy sugar crusts, and drank orange juice out of a paper carton. We sat on a rock outcropping in a fast breeze at almost the crest of a hill. Clouds flew through the deep green valleys below us and cows wandered in the grass.

A cow, perhaps a hundred yards away and directly in front of us, threw back her head. She began heaving herself toward us, awkwardly and rhythmically clomping across the turf.

"Why is that cow running toward us, Alex?"

"The cow isn't running at us. It probably doesn't even see us. Maybe it's trying to catch a bus."

The cow was running slowly but steadily, getting closer, bellowing and snorting. She was unmistakably aiming at us. The clouds continued to fly by.

"Alex, I think we should move. I really think we should get out of here."

"Why? I haven't finished my cake."

By now the cow had covered half the rock-speckled pasture between her and us.

"Alex, come on. It's coming right at us. It's after us." I pulled on his sleeve as panic rose in my throat. The cow was very big. If it fell on us, we'd be crushed.

Alex turned to look at me, and quietly chewed his cake. "Do you really think that a cow is trying to attack us?" He swallowed. "Why would it do that?"

By the tone of his voice, I knew he didn't see the situation the same way. I remained silent, deciding not to admit that I thought it was ready to trample me for my snacks. The cow kept coming, slowly, but relentless.

"It's still coming, Alex," I said.

"Lumpy, the cow is not after us. Cows don't attack."

She dipped below a small rise, but in a few seconds was visible again, still running directly toward us, now very close and making strained nasal sounds. I stood up.

"Oh my God, Alex, she is really coming!" I picked up the orange juice.

She disappeared again behind another little rise. In a moment, she emerged from the shelter of the hill heading back in the direction she came in, nudging along her calf that had strayed too close to the road.

I sat back down.

"Is there any juice left?" Alex asked. I handed him the carton. After thirty seconds or so he added, "It was good that you were ready, though. Good reflexes. We should face no danger from any more domesticated Spanish herbivores."

Two friends were once tormented for several hours by a

moose in the middle of the night in Wyoming. While they huddled in their sleeping bags, the moose circled and charged their tent for three hours. The moose's saliva leaked through the fabric and dripped onto their faces. He tossed their backpacks around the meadow they were camped in, covering them with snot. When they got back to town, the park ranger they spoke to suggested it was either jealousy or bugs: It was the rut, and the big blue tent might have been moving in on the moose's territory, or it was equally possible that the moose had been driven insane by biting insects. If it happened again, the ranger kindly suggested, they might try to find and get on top of a large boulder, one higher than the moose. Without letting the moose see them do it.

Consequently, a bovine attack didn't seem so unreasonable, but I didn't feel like arguing about it. We packed up our things and walked back to the road.

"I think that cow was packing," said Alex underneath his breath. He wasn't going to let this die.

"I'm not listening to you," I said.

"They have a real drug problem with younger cows around here. It's sad. Lot of them resort to prostitution with the deer."

"I'm really not listening."

"Makes them mad. Lots of mad cow in Europe. They strike in France all the time because French farmers don't warm their hands adequately before milking."

I looked at him. "Where do you come up with this stuff?"

AS WE TURNED a corner up at the top of the mountain, we heard a bell ringing. The sound felt like the wind that carried it, brisk and tingling, but sweet.

A few steps farther and a man waving a small brass hand-bell came into sight. He stood in the middle of the narrow street, surrounded by huge piles of rocks and roofless stone buildings, the abandoned town of Manjarín. He looked right at us with a smile. After a moment of confusion, I realized he was ringing the bell for us, ringing the bell to mark our arrival. "Welcome!" he shouted when we were perhaps twenty feet away from him, just next to a spotted horse tied to a wooden post and lazily chewing some grass.

We had arrived at Tomas's *refugio.*

"Please, rest. Would you like some coffee?" The thin young man with a leathered face, bright eyes, and round glasses ushered us to a wooden picnic table. It sat under a plastic awning outside a stone cottage. A group of five men stood a dozen feet away and spoke in whispers and angry exclamations. They shook their heads and sighed.

An eight-foot-tall wooden cross stood a few feet beyond the awning. Through the dark doorway into the cottage, I could barely glimpse what looked like benches and clothing and general dishevelment. A hand-painted sign above the doorway to the enclosed patio where we sat read, "Una Luz en el Camino," Light of the Camino.

"Would you like milk in your coffee? I have this milk here," the man motioned to a metal pitcher of foaming steamed milk, "but perhaps it is just a bit too cold. Let me make some more for you."

The coffee was hot and strong and delicious.

Another man walked quickly and deliberately from the cottage to the group of waiting men. He wore a white shirt with a large and pointed red cross that stretched almost from the neckline to the hem. He cleared his throat, unrolled what appeared to be a handwritten parchment scroll, and in a sonorous and booming voice, read Spanish I couldn't quite follow.

The group of men shouted their approval at different points during the reading and nodded their heads vigorously. The man rerolled his scroll, strode to his horse, jumped on, and took off down the road.

Alex and I watched in amazement.

"That was Tomas. He is the man who runs this *refugio,*" the man with the bell said.

We didn't really need to be told. It was obvious that whoever had just spoken and rode away was the man in charge, and we had learned that the man in charge was Tomas the night before when we stayed at a *refugio* run by the British Friends of the Camino. Victor, the English *refugio*-keeper there, told us about the man who ran a *refugio* in an abandoned town on the top of a mountain, living there year-round, even in ten feet of snow in winter. He believed it was his calling to run this *refugio* and care for pilgrims. He and his followers believed themselves to be modern-day Knights Templar. Victor clearly got a kick out of him, though was vaguely disapproving of what he considered the extremely unsanitary conditions of this *refugio* without running water, electricity, or sewage system.

"Oh, it's definitely worth stopping by, but I certainly wouldn't eat or drink anything let alone spend the night! But it is something to see!"

We were told by people who lived in the towns at the bottom of the mountain that Tomas's *refugio* was regularly shut down by the public health department in León for unsanitary conditions. That *refugio* was a health hazard! they cried. And now that the Camino was declared a world heritage sight by UNESCO,

Tomas wasn't just a local health hazard, but an international health hazard! He gave them all a bad name, living up there in a hovel, letting people from all over the world stay in a *refugio* with no plumbing or heating, as though all of northern Spain were so backward! And did you know that the last time the public health authorities demanded he close down, he rode his horse to León and staged a hunger strike until they relented! And did you know he thinks he is a knight, on a mission from God?

THE KNIGHTS TEMPLAR were medieval fighting monks, founded in Jerusalem during the Crusades, dedicated to protecting pilgrims traveling to holy places and to defeating or expelling infidels, namely the Moors, in Spain. They became incredibly powerful and wealthy, controlling lands and treasure all over Europe and the Middle East. Later on the Camino, we passed the ruins of a Templar castle, and it looked just like a fairy tale, with round turrets topped by spiky walls and a moat. Eventually, the Knights Templar's power became their undoing. In the early fourteenth century, King Philip the Fair of France accused the order of heresy and sacrilege, most likely in order to get their land. The pope at the time, Clement V, was weak and ineffectual, and acquiesced. The monks were arrested and brutally tortured. Many of them, including the Grand Master Jacques de Molay, admitted to committing heretical acts in their secret chapter meetings. The Order's possessions were seized and redistributed. When Jacques de Molay was sentenced for heresy in front of Notre Dame Cathedral, he interrupted the proceedings, and declared his innocence, recanting his earlier confession made under torture and decrying the actions of Philip and Clement. He was immediately sentenced to burn at the stake as a lapsed heretic. Less than a year later, both king and pope died. Legend spread that they were called before God to answer for their crimes against the innocent Knights.

Legends still flourish about the Order today, and conspiracy theories abound. They range from the idea that the fraternal society of Freemasons are descended not from stonemasons in England, as their name would imply, but rather from English Knights in hiding, to the idea that the Knights Templar's role of protecting pilgrims was only secondary to their real calling, which was to protect the hundreds of blood descendants of Jesus and his wife, Mary Magdalen, descendants the Roman Catholic Church has spent thousands of years and much spilled blood to keep secret.

Tomas is not the only person today who thinks of himself as a modern-day Knight Templar. An Internet search will turn up the Web sites of all sorts of modern incarnations, including a branch of the masons who call themselves Knights Templar and even dress as they imagine the original Knights did. As far as I could tell, though, they didn't actually do any pilgrim protecting, instead funneling their good deeds to a foundation on eye diseases.

Tomas, whether or not he literally thought of himself as a Knight Templar, certainly took the idea of caring for pilgrims seriously.

It was easy to be skeptical of Tomas's *refugio,* as some people were—with its lack of sanitation, Tomas's impassioned charges into town to protest injustice, and the quixotic attempt to resurrect a band of fighting monks in an abandoned town. Knight or not, called by God or not, I'll never know. It's between God and Tomas. All I can say about his work is that we stopped at many beautiful *refugios* along the way, with kind people who welcomed us and comforted us. We met hundreds of generous people who made up this remarkable community of the Camino. But no one ever made me feel like that smiling man that day. To realize he was ringing that bell for no one else but me and Alex—no one had ever rung a bell for me before or since—pealing out the joyful news that we were approaching as though I was an important person, a priceless person for whom bells are rung, as though I was the lost sheep the shepherd searched for, as though I were beloved.

26.

The Camino was in deep shade as it meandered through town. Unlike most, this little village seemed to lack a central plaza. Giant dense trees arched overhead, and their twisted roots curled across the Camino. Nothing grew on the densely shaded ground, and so the Camino was not really a clear path but rather a packed dirt track through loamy and springy dirt. Sitting on the stone steps of a house right on the Camino were two old men. Both were missing several teeth and both had thinning white hair that flopped around as they moved their heads. Both had red gin blossoms spreading across their noses and cheeks, but one was tall and thin and the other short and pudgy.

The tall one shouted out hello as we passed, while the short one giggled. We said hello back, and immediately the tall one asked where we were from as the short one stared. It seemed rude to keep walking as they spoke to us, and so we stopped to answer.

The tall, thin one who was clearly the leader, and his short supportive sidekick, made space on the steps and asked us to sit. Alex and I glanced at each other, and then we both began to shake our heads, back up, and say that we really must be going, but the tall one grabbed both our wrists and began to tug at us, and so in order not to cause a scene we sat. Alex was next to the short one and I sat next to the tall.

He asked me if I liked being a pilgrim, but didn't wait for an answer. He had something to say, and I was his captive audience. He said he did not believe in religion, he did not believe in Christianity, and so he did not believe in pilgrimage, though all the pilgrims he met were nice people, he reassured me. Did I know why he did not believe in religion? And before I could answer, he told me. It was because of what happened in his life he said with a shout, and he grabbed my upper arm.

He grew up Catholic, right in that little town, and he grew up going to church, and knowing about the pilgrimage, and with a statue of Mary in his bedroom. He had nothing against religion then, he said emphatically, touching my arm again, because religion was just something in his life, like eating breakfast. He didn't really notice it. Did I know what made him realize that religion was a sham, that religion was dangerous, that religion was wrong? His voice rose and cracked as he asked the question, and his previously slurred words became clear. I remained silent, expecting him to tell me, but this time he waited for a response. He nudged my arm to try to elicit an answer. No, I didn't know what happened to him.

Franco! He boomed, his alcoholic breath spreading over my face. He again grabbed my arm. Franco happened to him and to his family and his town and to Spain. And he would never believe in religion again. For two reasons, he explained: If Franco believed something, it must be wrong, and Franco had embraced Catholicism as no one he had ever seen. And he had seen what evil could be done in the name of religion, and so he wanted nothing to do with it. Nothing!

I could smell the alcohol not only on his breath but in his sweat as well, and see it in his unstable, swaying body. I didn't want to anger him. The tingle down my spine warned that he was possibly violent. I was looking for a graceful exit out of the conversation. I peeked over to see how Alex was doing. He was laughing, carrying on a conversation in English with an old drunk who spoke only Spanish. Neither understood the other, but they seemed to be having a great time. Neither was yelling about Franco, but the old man was waving his hands around, telling a story that Alex seemed to find funny.

The thin old man grabbed my arm again to get my attention. What did I think of what he had to say?

I didn't know how to answer him. I had sensed enough from the few weeks we'd spent in Spain to know that this was a volatile topic, and not one I wanted to tread on because I knew so little about what life was like for this man and Spain under Franco. I didn't know what role religion had played in the pain he so clearly felt. Religion, the constellation of practices, beliefs, and institutional structures, was a very different creature in Spain than it was in the United States. I was in foreign territory. Religion in Spain, it was clear everywhere we went, has long been wrapped up in politics, in suffering, and in violence. The questions of religion and power and violence and belief are almost impossible to get away from on the Camino, where bloody crucifixes and even bloodier representations of martyrdom grace countless churches, and where statues of a giant, scowling Saint James decapitating Moors and crushing their heads under his horse's hooves loom from the second story of buildings.

In a church museum, a painting of the death of a martyr depicted the man flayed but still alive. He stood before a crowd holding his skin thrown jauntily over his shoulder like a suit jacket while his striated magenta muscles oozed blood and his eyeballs bulged from their sockets. This painting was the last in a series of paintings depicting the life and death of this saint. The pictures of his earthly ministry were bland and forgettable, but the scenes of his slow, tortuous death were painted with great detail, high color, and undeniable emotion. Martyrdom was the thing revered. A grisly death made the saint, not a pious life, seemed to be the message in much of Spanish religious art.

The glorification of violence is not limited to violence visited upon a saint. Sometimes the praise is for violence a saint visits on others. Saint James is celebrated as the patron saint of Spain because he was believed to have preached there before his death, but also because of the miracles of Santiago Matamoras—Saint James the killer of Moors. Images of Matamoras, from postcards to marble statues, depict a "miracle" that occurred in the fifteenth century, when the Christians of the Iberian peninsula fought the Muslims for control of the land. As the Christians battled to drive the Moors back to Africa and were losing in a critical fight, the telling of the miracle goes, Saint James thundered in from the sky on a white charger, and single-handedly killed thousands of Muslims, turning the tide of the battle to victory for the Christians.

The defeat of the Moors and the Christian control of the peninsula marks the beginning of Spain as a unified country. It also allowed for the eventual flourishing of the Inquisition, the forced conversion or expulsion of Jews, and, some historians argue, for the historic basis of racism, an ideology based not so much on skin color as on religious heritage. Violence, religion, politics, martyrdom, nationalism all swirled together. Impossible to ignore, but it was, and is, hard for me to make sense of.

He grabbed my arm again. "You did not answer me!" he yelled. But as soon as I opened my mouth, he began talking again, gesticulating forcefully, grabbing my arm when he wanted to make a point. He continued his speech for another three minutes or so. Then, just as I noticed he was touching me a little too often, bam! He made his move. The tall, thin old man grabbed my right breast, the whole palm right on it. And it couldn't have been a mistake, because his fingers closed around and gave me a soft squeeze.

I jumped right up, knocking him off balance.

"We have to go! Right now!" I said to Alex, who, still carrying on his happily indecipherable conversation with the short, fat man, said, "Okay." He stood up, leaving his conversation partner mid-sentence.

"Oh, you must come back to my house for some lunch. My wife will make us sandwiches. We were having a good talk," the short one said, reaching out to grab Alex's hand.

"No, we have to go."

The tall, thin man looked down sheepishly, and when he began to look up, I turned away and would not look at him.

When we were a few yards away Alex asked what happened. I told him that in the midst of his diatribe on Franco and the dangers of religious violence, the tall one grabbed my breast.

A wide grin broke out on Alex's face.

"I wondered when he was going to make his move," he said.

"What? You don't think that was funny, do you?"

"Well, yeah, I mean, no. No, that is not funny at all. I can't believe he did that. It's terrible. Terrible." He tried to look somber. "But, you do have to admit, it's pretty funny. We're on this religious pilgrimage, and some old drunk wants to give a history lesson on Franco and religion, being all serious, but when he sees an opportunity, he makes a grab for it. You know?"

I tried to look offended and hurt. My patient, two-backpack carrying boyfriend and companion was apparently pro–sexual assault.

He noticed my look, and as he tends to do, kept trying to clarify before I started yelling. "It's like, 'Hey, that religion thing is really working out for you, buddy. Way to go.' People, you know, no matter how lofty they act or talk, all they really want is food and booty. It's the same everywhere. So you have to be forgiving, I guess."

"That's your advice? All people are motivated by food and sex?" I asked.

"Yeah. People don't want to be hungry or alone. What else is there?"

"That's a beautiful religion you've made yourself. Brilliant."

He grinned at me. "You can be my head saint—Mother Hotness of the Bodacious Ta Ta. You'd be sort of like Saint Lucy but a lot more entertaining for everybody."

I shook my head. We walked on for a few yards in silence.

"I can go back and thrash him if you want," he said.

"We're on a pilgrimage," I answered.

"Probably inappropriate?"

I nodded and readjusted my backpack on my shoulders.

Alex said, "Maybe we could get a *cello* for it. A stamp of a big fist flattening an old Spaniard."

"I swear, Alex, one day I really am going to hit you with my shoe," I said. "But thank you for offering to beat up an old man. Very chivalrous."

"I do what I can."

We continued down the road.

27.

It was a cool and overcast day. A gentle drizzle came on and off, but was never strong enough to require a rain jacket. My battered baseball cap, which had turned from white to a sweat-stained mottled brown, was enough protection. The misty air clung to our skin just enough to cool us off but not enough to get us wet. It was a beautiful day.

The part of Spain we were now in was damp and green and soft. The Camino traveled through forests of chestnut trees as wide as houses. On open hillsides, the overwhelmingly sweet scent of the yellow flowers scattered across the scrub was so strong it stung.

We walked slowly but steadily. The panic-driven speed of the first half of the pilgrimage had subsided, and before we knew it, we had walked twenty kilometers before two o'clock in the afternoon and arrived at the *refugio* we had chosen for the day.

It was in a tiny little town, if it could be called that. Unlike every other town on the Camino, where the demarcation between town and fields was startlingly clear, Alex and I didn't realize we had reached the town until we were in the middle of it. The Camino here didn't follow the auto road, as it had been doing for much of the past few days. We came out of a forest into a clearing of knee-high, swaying grasses and wildflowers, with a crumbling stone church on the horizon.

The building was locked and I couldn't tell if it was even used as a church anymore, because the windows were too dusty to see through. The walled-off courtyard in front of the church's front door was unkempt, littered with stones and weeds. About a dozen yards away and up a gentle slope, behind a stone wall, crooked headstones with soft, curved edges erupted from the earth amid the flowers and grasses. They looked as though they were growing out of the dirt, too, as though they had been turned from limestone into something organic, something that didn't melt into the ground with the rain but gently unfurled from it. I wanted to walk around in those headstones and flowers, but I suppose the place had that effect on a lot of people, because the iron gate was locked shut.

It seemed to be an abandoned church slowly crumbling back into the fields, with no signs of human life anywhere, but when we walked around a corner and past a stand of trees, there was the *refugio* we had planned to stay in that night. It was a two-story white cement building that looked no more than ten or fifteen years old, swarming with people. A dozen pilgrims were standing around the front door, and a dozen more were walking around in the packed-down dirt yard. Backpacks were scattered and piled like rock outcroppings, and at least two people were hanging from each window, their entire torsos leaning into the air.

A smiling and round-cheeked girl called out to us from the second story, "I think the *refugio* is full, but you might want to try over in that cow shed." She pointed to a small, open-sided concrete lean-to half-hidden in the brush off to the left.

We turned and watched a group of twenty teenagers emerge

from the trees, descend upon the cow shed in a hooting, running, jumping mass, and claim it as their own.

After a moment the girl turned back to us and said, "Maybe there's still room on the kitchen floor."

Sleeping bags, backpacks, and bodies littered every bit of horizontal surface. The kitchen floor was already taken. The *refugio*-keeper, a flustered young man trailing a swarm of pilgrims, suggested we call a cab to take us back to Sarria, the large town we had passed through just five kilometers back.

We had taken a bus and a train, but at no time had it occured to me that we could have called a cab. All that time in the wheat fields, all those afternoons where I almost drove Alex to running away in the middle of the night, all those meltdowns—and we could have borrowed a cell phone and called a taxi.

A pay phone stood all by itself in the middle of the dirt clearing. As far as we could tell, this was the whole town—the *refugio,* the abandoned church, and the pay phone. I was afraid that the cab company back in Sarria would have no idea where we were, but the dispatcher knew just the place I was talking about and cheerfully assured us a car would be there in less than ten minutes.

As the taxi pulled up and Alex and I gathered our bags, a group of four middle-aged Frenchmen walked over to the car, and started to open the back door. I politely tried to tell them that we had called for the cab, but they just smiled and began to get in.

"Mother of God! What the Hell?" Alex yelled in a combination of Spanish and English. He stalked over to them, waving his arms as if trying to shoo them away. I recognized the gesture as one the bank manager used during Alex's ATM attack. Apparently he thought it was some sort of international symbol for anger. "You had better not fucking try to snake our cab!" From the tone of his voice, I realized Alex had reached the end of his remarkable patience when it came to middle-aged Frenchmen. He looked like he was about to tackle someone. The four men looked at Alex, then me, and backed off.

The cabbie sped us out on the twisting one-lane road to a small highway. Within five minutes we were back in Sarria.

"The *refugio* here is already full," the driver told us, which we had known when we passed through two hours before. "Is there some hotel you want to go to?"

When we answered we had no idea, he told us he knew of a nice and cheap hotel with rooms available and dropped us off. With a wave, he made a three-point turn and told us he was headed right back out to the *refugio*. There would be a line of pilgrims waiting for a cab, he said with glee.

It seemed as though overnight the Camino became full of people. A steady stream of people had always been walking through, and we always saw other pilgrims at the *refugios* and restaurants. But during the first few weeks and the first few hundred kilometers, there were days when we saw no other pilgrims between setting out in the morning and settling down in the evening. Now it was a rare occasion to be by ourselves for even an hour at a time. The Camino was crowded because we were so close to Santiago, and according to the guidelines of the pilgrimage, a person only has to walk the last hundred kilometers to qualify for the much-coveted Compostela.

Alex and I had no idea how desired that Compostela certificate was until we went to get ours, *credenciales* in hand. The cathedral of Santiago has a special office set up for the granting of the certificates, and while there we saw several people try to get a Compostela though they had not walked any of the Camino, having instead done it by tour bus. One woman burst into tears when denied a Compostela. It was not fair, she cried. She had driven the car, bought the groceries, and toted around the backpacks for her husband and his friends for two weeks, while they walked the requisite mileage. She should get a Compostela for her work, too. None of the men would have been able to finish the Camino if she had not ferried around their belongings, stopping every few kilometers with cold drinks and fresh sandwiches for them by the side of the road. She was denied.

The Camino was crowded now, and it wasn't possible to be solitary. The feeling of it changed. The intimacy of the earlier Camino was gone, when we knew most of the pilgrims at least by face, but in its place was a joviality and playfulness that hadn't been there when the pilgrims were more sparse. We heard many pilgrims, especially those who had walked all the way from France or even farther, complain that the Camino was now too crowded, but in some ways the crowded road and towns and *refugios* were really more in the spirit of what the Camino once was. Many thousands of people walked or bicycled the last hundred kilometers to Santiago the summer we walked the Camino, but six hundred years earlier, many hundreds of thousands would have arrived.

The Camino was now populated with whole families walking the pilgrimage, and children as pilgrims made their first appearances. Church youth groups of teenagers in matching bandannas could be heard from kilometers away as they sang and shouted while walking along. The newer pilgrims adopted the iconography of medieval pilgrimage with a gusto that no one starting in Roncesvalles displayed. It would have been next to impossible to make it all the way carrying the things the newer pilgrims loved—tall wooden canes with fake gourds attached by leather straps; broad, floppy burlap hats; and real scallop shells the size of a hand around their necks, which bounced against their breastbones with every step. The staffs slapped against the floor incessantly as they were dropped by their owners or slid down the walls they were propped against. It was a noise as startling as a gunshot, and it echoed through *refugios*, churches, cafés, in the streets, everywhere. Many of the newer pilgrims approached the pilgrimage with a sense of festival, dress-up, or play, something that had been missing before. Their behavior pointed out that there was another aspect of pilgrimage. It wasn't all athletic endurance test or serious meditation. Sometimes pilgrimage was getting drunk and singing all night with a bunch of strangers, which we did quite a bit toward the end.

But never before had we walked to a town and found nowhere to stay. And much to my surprise, I wasn't bothered by this at all. Four weeks earlier, I would have had a panic attack, but now it seemed to be a small price to pay for how much fun we were having.

The feeling on the Camino had changed, from a lonely trek through the vast, open, and unknown places of mind and land to a crowded party, a sense of expectation, excitement, looking forward. It changed from a feeling of distressed introspection, of fear of what was lurking in my own mind to betray me, to the warm feeling of Thanksgiving night, once dessert is over and everyone is playing board games, a strength and comfort in the people around you, a feeling of not being alone.

PART 10

Grieving

28.

We came to a complete stop while walking. For once, it was too difficult to walk and chew at the same time. We'd bought a pint of raspberries at a farmer's stand along the side of the road and they were the best thing I had ever eaten. Ever. And I've eaten a lot.

Alex was already way ahead of me in consumption, shoving berries in his mouth as fast as his pink-stained hands would move. We ate a pint of raspberries in less than half a minute. The sugary juice ran down to my elbow and dripped off my chin.

When the last raspberry was gone we scooped up all the remaining berry bits with our fingertips. I licked the carton.

"I think we need to get some more," Alex said.

We turned around to walk back to the woman who had sold us the berries. She had turned around, too, and was looking at us, waiting, knowing just what we would do.

She was sitting in a lawn chair on the side of the Camino, which was also the main road through the tiny town. She had a card table spread out in front of her, covered with parcels. It was a soft day, the kind of day when the temperature seems to match your body temperature perfectly, and the air has no feeling against your skin.

When we had approached her the first time, she stood and said hello. Her table was covered in plastic pint cartons filled with raspberries and cloth-covered circles. She picked one up and peeled the thin cloth back to reveal a pale wheel of cheese. She made them herself, she explained. The cheese was beautiful and smelled sweet and pungent at the same time. But who wants to carry around five pounds of cheese? We went for the raspberries.

"Do you want sugar on them?" she asked as she held up a brown paper bag.

"No, I don't think so," I said.

"Yes, you do," she nodded encouragingly. "Trust me. How about on just half of them?"

I watched, astounded as she poured at least a cup of sugar over half the carton. She was, of course, right. The sugar on the super-ripe berries turned them into something even more perfect than they already were.

She was expecting us to return and nodded when we stood again in front of her table.

We asked for two more cartons.

"With sugar," she said. A laugh, loud and gruff, erupted from her belly. Halfway through pouring sugar on the second pint, she ran out. She waved at us to follow her, and then brought us through the little wood door behind her, set into a high stone wall.

Inside her courtyard, row after row of raspberry brambles were neatly divided by stone paths, and a tabby cat sunned himself. She pointed to the garden with pride.

"I pick them all myself," she said and held up her rough maroon hands. On a work table under the eave were thirty more cartons of berries, ten more wheels of cheese, and a dozen more bags of white sugar.

We met up with a Spanish man just a few meters after leaving the woman's little stand. "Oh, that will make you sick," he warned and shook his head. But they didn't make me sick, and they didn't make Alex sick.

It was also cherry season in that part of Spain, and as we walked we saw families on ladders and in red-speckled trees, picking fruit. Even little children perched precariously on the tops of ladders, while their grandmothers sorted the buckets of cherries below and sold them at tables along the way.

We bought some cherries the next day from a woman set up in the shade. To her left was a hip-high plastic barrel of cherries, and a cardboard box of plastic bags sat at her right. The only things on the table were a big metal scoop and an old-fashioned metal balancing scale, with its big empty bowl swaying gently on its thin chains.

"You want cherries?" she asked.

"Yes, please."

"How much?"

Somehow I wasn't expecting that question. I turned to look at Alex. I had no idea how much to order, realizing instantly that I had never bought cherries before. "What do you think?"

"I don't know." He leaned back slightly. He looked shocked and almost offended that I asked him, looking as though he thought I was trying to blame him for something.

"Well, I don't know either . . ."

"A kilo?" the woman asked. She nodded when we both looked at her confused.

"A kilo?" I repeated to Alex.

"How many cherries are in a kilo?" Alex backed up a step.

"I don't know. I don't know how much a kilo is."

"A kilo?" she asked one more time while Alex and I looked

at each other and then back at her again, blankly. "A kilo," the woman said definitively with a bright smile, and she started to scoop cherries into a bag. A lot of cherries. A kilo is 2.2 pounds of cherries in a plastic bag. That is more than two people really want to eat. As she shoveled and shoveled cherries, and the scale moved ever so slowly, I realized we would be eating cherries for days. Alex just gazed off in the distance, as though he didn't notice what was going on.

She hefted the bulging bag off the scale and swung it across the table to us.

"Huh." Alex held up the bag at arms' length and gazed at it intently. "We better start eating."

I ate a dozen cherries then. I ate some more after dinner that night, and again in the morning, but after that, I was done with the cherries. My stomach turned at the thought of eating any more. All I could think about were those raspberries in sugary raspberry juice. Alex had to eat all the cherries himself.

He pushed on, and carried around the two-pound bag, dutifully pulling it out and eating some fruit every time we stopped for a break. He would pull out the rustling plastic bag, take a deep breath, and reach into it. He would lie in bed at night, sigh, and pop the cherries into his mouth until he couldn't stand it anymore, and then wake up the next morning and eat cherries before breakfast. He was not going to throw those cherries out, and he was determined to eat them all before any went bad. After a couple days, he looked at the bag mournfully, eyes downcast and shoulders bowed. By the end of the bag, after four days of almost nonstop cherries, he would shudder before eating each one. He doesn't eat cherries now.

I asked at every farm stand along the way and in every town, but no one else we saw along the Camino sold raspberries. Cherries just could not compare, in my mouth and mind.

A FRIEND OF mine once said, as he held up a tangerine, that the only thing that allowed him to believe in God when he had been diagnosed with multiple sclerosis was fruit. It was the most perfect thing in the world, he said, beautiful and delicious, and healthy for you at the same time it effectively fulfilled its purpose, to help plants reproduce. Everything worked together perfectly, all those different animals and plants helping each other. And it came in its own perfect packaging. Not even the most brilliant human mind could think up such a thing, he thought. He could not give up all belief in a good and wise and creative God because he had fruit. And he had never eaten those raspberries.

I think sometimes you have to hang on to whatever you can when it comes to faith. And if that's fruit, so be it. There are times in at least some people's lives—maybe many people—when belief in any compassionate or kind or even benign force in the universe is almost impossible. But if you can just hold on to something—or perhaps more likely, if something holds on to you—it can be the beginning of a new way of seeing, a new life.

29.

"What are you mumbling about?" Alex asked as we crossed a creek that smelled of cayenne pepper and rotten eggs.

"Oh, I was just praying my intention for the pilgrimage."

"What is it?"

"I don't want to say. I'll jinx myself."

"Is that official doctrine or something you made up in your neuroses?"

I shot him what I hoped was a withering look. "I haven't gotten an answer yet and we're almost there so I'm getting worried."

"You? Worried?"

"Well, what's your intention?"

It was much the same question Madame de Bril asked at the very beginning of the trip. Ideally, an intention for a pilgrimge is supposed to be to give thanks, or to ask for one of the traditional spiritual gifts, like patience or strength or love or humility, some key aspect to life that you lack. Everyone we met, though, was asking for specific, tangible things. One woman wanted a high-paying, enjoyable job back in Barcelona, and fully expected to have an answering machine full of job offers when she returned home. Saint James had driven the Moors out of Spain after centuries of domination, hadn't he? What then was a job search to him? Another couple were praying for a baby, and an auto mechanic wanted to find a wife, though as he got closer to Santiago, he had to start to admit to himself that he might not find her right on the Camino itself, as he had expected.

"I don't have one. I'm just walking along. So what's yours? Maybe I can help you figure it out."

"Well, I was asking God what I should do with my life. Some career advice so I would know what classes to take in the fall."

I'd been praying in a singsong way, "Please please please please let me figure out what to do with my life." And then I would go over my options, but the only thing I could come up with that sounded good was ballerina. And for that I would need to lose thirty-five pounds, develop a sense of balance, and somehow get my arches to lift an inch and a half. Since I was somehow gaining weight walking fifteen miles a day and tripped over my feet regularly, this didn't seem likely.

"I'm a little nervous because we're only three days outside of Santiago and I still don't know what the answer is."

Alex stopped and looked at me, letting his backpack slide down his shoulders so the straps rested on his elbows. This was a good technique for letting the steam escape from your sopping-wet back. "Did you expect it to be spray-painted on a rock or something?" He raised an eyebrow.

"Well, I don't know. I mean, Moses got a burning bush."

I wanted a road map, a clear path to follow, and clear directions on how to proceed each step of the way. I never got the answer I was looking for. No clear and concise career advice was forthcoming.

But I did get *an* answer. I didn't need career counseling; I needed to be cracked open—by walking, by breathing, by beauty, by anger, by joy, by love. Like a morning glory seed whose shell is so hard it has to be soaked in water before it can start to grow, I needed to be cracked open to grieve. To sense God. The Camino was just the very beginning of grief, the opening volley of a few years of making new sense out of life and the world. But all along, there had been a sense that I was not seeing what I should be, that I was somehow missing something right in front of my face.

ON A WINDY March morning, two months before we left for Spain, I walked through campus holding on to the thin white rope that cordoned off the verboten grass as though I needed it to guide me from one place to another. I ran into a friend who could see I wasn't doing too well, and she suggested I call a woman she once heard speak. "I don't know why, but I think she could really help you," she said. But she only knew the woman's first name, Sister Jeannette, and nothing else. An hour later I met another friend for lunch, and mentioned this to her.

"I've met her! She runs a hospice for former prisoners and is a spiritual director. She's wonderful. I don't know her phone number or where she works, but I bet you could find it pretty easily."

That night I ran into a fellow student I barely knew in the lobby of our apartment building. I mentioned to her that I was going to try to find a woman named Sister Jeannette.

"I work for her," she interrupted. "I can give you her phone number right now." She promptly wrote it in red ink on yellow paper.

JEANNETTE WAS SHORT and a bit round, with white hair that refused to lie flat on her head, and round glasses. She moved with perfect efficiency and confidence. I felt a bit out of control walking next to her.

We sat in a tiny room in the basement of the church, with two plush armchairs and a table with a lamp that cast a faint light in the dark room. The darkness and smallness, and the presence of this woman who had hugged me when we first met—a real hug, not a fake, angle in and pat each other on the back hug—made the room feel like a little cocoon where I could curl up.

Jeannette didn't suggest that suffering has a purpose, as I had heard from many people, or that the mystery of creation is not something we can understand. She just said she disagreed with my understanding of God generally.

"I don't think God chooses to make people sick. I don't think he singled out your father. I don't think God functions the way you seem to think," she said.

She didn't think God *was* what I thought. Maybe the picture of God I developed as I grew up wasn't so accurate. It certainly wasn't her view.

"Well, what do you think God is like?"

"I have a special devotion to the Holy Spirit. I really try to watch for the Spirit in my life, to see how God works in my life. I try to pay attention to it."

This idea of the Holy Spirit always baffled me. It was mentioned in prayers in church, and I'd learned somewhere along the way that it was some vague, mysterious force of God that landed on the apostles after Jesus' ascension in the New Testament, and made little flames sprout out the tops of their heads, but in all my growing up Catholic, no one ever bothered to tell me how this thing might have anything to do with my life right now. Certainly, no one ever suggested I could have a special devotion to it.

"But how do you know it's the Holy Spirit?" I asked. "What are you talking about when you say that?"

She paused for a few seconds and tilted her head a bit to the side. "Well, I guess what other people would call coincidence, I would call the Holy Spirit."

Was it coincidence that I bumped into three people who knew this woman on one afternoon, and that the last could jot down her number on a piece of paper, literally handing me the way to contact her? I had thought it was lucky coincidence. I liked this idea about coincidence not being just coincidence but instead being the gentle hand of the Spirit, but I was also skeptical. What about unlucky coincidences? What about coincidences that didn't lead to good things but to pain or death or suffering?

"You'll just have to start paying attention for yourself," she replied. "Just see what you see, and let yourself be open to seeing."

The next week, she changed the subject.

"I've been thinking that it might really help you to go to therapy, to try to work out some of your grief issues. You seem stuck."

"Absolutely not." I was appalled. I was fine emotionally, didn't she see that? Remember, I was feeling nothing at this point. I just had some questions about God. Why did everyone think grieving was my problem when I knew for certain my problem was with God?

My problem *was* with God, but this is because, for me, there wasn't such a difference between God and grieving, between mourning and praying. I definitely had a problem with grief, too, but I didn't see it then. I wanted God explained to me, but I couldn't know anything about God because I could not mourn, and I could not grieve because to grieve is to draw so close to God that it's as if you were throwing yourself into God's arms, and I was afraid and angry and confused by God. Sister Jeannette and I were both right; my problem was with God and my problem was with grief, because they could not be separated.

IF PRAYER IS the attempt to understand God, then grieving is the deepest form of prayer, rising from the body and soul and mind, asking God and really and truly wanting to know, no matter what the answer: Who are you? Why did you create a world with pain? Why is life this way? What are you? Because you are not what I thought you were.

Grieving, at its deepest level, is to acknowledge that creation can be cruel and that people suffer. To look at this truth, to allow yourself to feel it, you are forced to consider the nature of this world and this existence. You ask how this can be and who set this up and why this happens. To grieve is to ask God the hardest questions. To grieve is to ask who God really is. It's to change your perspective on all other human beings and their relationships to one another and to you and your place in this world. To grieve is to start over, to be re-created.

It was the wounds of grief—gaping, bloody gashes into my neatly ordered view of the world and of God—that allowed a new understanding of God to seep in, and not one of my own making alone, but one drawn in from the sun and the wheat and the mud and the holy chickens and Felicia and her dog and everyone and everything else on that pilgrimage. It was in pain, broken down, that I first allowed myself to get a glimpse of God, or perhaps God let me have a glimpse of Godself. Or perhaps it's that I finally recognized what had been all around me all the time but had not noticed, because I was expecting something or someone else. This is what I did not understand about the ascetics—that many of them got this and were trying to open themselves up to God more and more. I may not agree with their methods, but it wasn't just self-hatred for them. They drank the pus of the wounds of the sick because they recognized that grace pours through this woundedness. It was both the grief and the realization of joy despite the grief, joy within grief, and ultimately joy as always and ever co-existing with grief, that allowed me to notice how God is present.

There are some remarkable paintings and prints of the crucified Christ that depict beautiful flowers growing out of his pierced hands and feet and the gash in his side. They can be disturbing, but they make sense to me now. New life through wounds. Grace through grief. And maybe that's why the artist of the bloody crucifix in the octagonal church loved those drops of blood that resembled poppies and the twisted body that resembled wheat. In the very geography of his life was grace. Blood and poppies and wheat and flesh were all prayer.

It still doesn't answer the question, though, the classic question of theology and human searching, of why the painful things happen in the first place. How could there be a God of cool shade in a world in which pain is just part of the deal, in which it is just going to happen no matter what? Why suffering? Why grief? And why grief and God?

I don't know. I'm not sure anyone does.

For my thoughts are not your thoughts,
and your ways are not my ways, says the Lord.
As high as the heavens are above the earth,
So high are my ways above your ways
And my thoughts above your thoughts.
—Isaiah 55:8–9

PART 11

Wonder

30.

The day before we planned to arrive in Santiago was hot and still, but we walked through tall forests of eucalyptus trees. They didn't cast much shade because they were so tall and skinny and their leaves were thin and long, but I liked the smell as I walked so I didn't mind the lack of shade. In the morning, we walked past three men who were cutting down some of the trees. A man stepped out into the path and held up his hand as though he were stopping traffic. He didn't say anything, and after a loud crack and what sounded like a flurry of papers falling off a desk, a tree toppled sideways, and he waved us on.

We stayed at a little inn that night, and while Alex napped in the afternoon, I bought two honey-glazed doughnuts wrapped in cellophane in the bar. I sat outside in a lawn chair in the sun and ate them. They had melted a little in the heat and much of the honey ended up on the plastic wrapping, so I had to lick the cellophane. It did not occur to me to wonder what finishing the pilgrimage would be like. I like to think that I was completely living in the moment, in a Zen Buddhist–like state of meditation, blissful in the present, not longing for the past or hoping for the future. But I think that, in reality, at least a little part of my mind was in denial.

The last day of the pilgrimage dawned bright and, of course, hot. This was tolerable at first, but as the day wore on, and as we got closer to the end, and I realized that if some great epiphany of knowledge and understanding was going to occur, it had to be today, I got it into my mind that I needed it to be cool and misty in order to end this properly, in order to finally figure out and settle and put in place all the things that were going on in my head. Cool and misty was the key, but the entire region of Galicia was experiencing one of its hottest and driest summers that any of the people who lived along the Camino could remember, and this day was one of the brightest and hottest of that summer so far. By the time we reached Santiago, I was fighting the panic that was beginning to radiate out from my diaphragm. This wasn't going to work. This was all going to be for nothing. I would have walked (and taken the train and the bus) all this way in this sun for nothing. My mouth and eyes began to cry against my will.

Just outside of the city, the Camino crosses beneath a big elevated highway—shade. I threw off the backpack and sat on a rock in the great expanse of dirt and gravel under the bridge.

"I don't want to go any farther. Let's just get a taxi."

"Oh my God, I can't believe we are doing this on the last day," Alex said.

"What is that supposed to mean?"

"You know exactly what that means. You cannot flag down a taxi. You have to finish this."

I didn't answer.

"A school bus just went by, and you know what? Those kids were laughing at you."

"Oh, whatever, Alex. Those kids were not laughing at me."

"Yeah, they were. Laughing at the pilgrim who decided a hundred yards away from finishing that she needed a cab, sprawled out on a dirty rock below an underpass that smells like donkey piss. I'd laugh, too, if I didn't actually have to live this moment."

So as not to give in immediately, I sat on the rock for a few minutes while Alex walked ahead. And as so often was the case those five weeks, I then had to walk even faster to catch up to him.

It was easy to obsess over the fact that the very last day of the pilgrimage was as hot and miserable as the darkest days in the middle. Much easier to think about that than to ponder that I would soon have to fly back to Massachusetts and try to figure out how this experience could fit in with a regular life. Mostly, I think, I was afraid that it couldn't, that the sense of peace and acceptance and this feeling of a loving, playful, strong, and always there God only existed in Spain. Perhaps God didn't live in American cities the way God lived in rural Spain along an old pilgrimage road.

As we walked up to the massive steps leading into the cathedral, all I focused on was how cool and shady it would be inside the church.

We walked through the ornate iron gates and up the steps, following the crowd because neither of us knew what to do at that point. The crowd stopped and formed into lines, and as Alex explained one does in Russia, when you see a line, you get on it. I stood on my toes to try to see what was up there, but all I could see were the backs of people's heads.

The line moved slowly. I thought about how cold it must be in the church and how I would like to lie down on the marble floor. I thought about Sno-Cones and icy sodas. I thought about Pizza Hut. Surely a town this big would have a Pizza Hut. I would have gotten off the line and walked past whatever everyone was waiting to see except that I couldn't. The line blocked the doors. So I stood. Alex was much better at standing in line than I was.

Finally we passed through the wrought-iron gates and double wood doors and into a vestibule. The line ended very shortly ahead of us, and people were waiting in front of a pillar holding up the double arches leading into the church, staring at it intently. It was a Tree of Jesse, a sculpted pillar upon which the entire tympanum seemed to rest. The twisting sculpture traced all of humankind from Adam through Mary, topped by a large sculpture of Jesus. People were walking up to it, one at a time. Each person put her hand on the pillar, bowed three times, and then stuck her right hand in what looked like the mouth of a fish down by one's knees. Some people began to cry and some began to laugh when they touched the tree, and some just looked startled. I couldn't tell what they were reacting to. From where I stood it just looked like a run-of-the-mill Tree of Jesse, just like any of the dozens all over churches in Europe.

I walked up when it was my turn, aware that I had no idea what I was doing or why. My armpits began to prickle. I had no idea how to do this, not just at the sculpture but at this whole point—I had no idea how to end a pilgrimage. I didn't want it to end, and hadn't stopped to think what it would be like or how I was supposed to do it. I liked being a pilgrim (when I didn't hate being a pilgrim). It was so orderly, so secure. I woke up in the morning and ate some bread and drank coffee. Then we started walking. Ate lunch. Walked some more. Ate dinner. Went to bed. Slept. Woke up and ate some bread. I felt so much safer than I did in Massachusetts. I was afraid that the crushing dread would return. I did not know how not to be Kerry who wasn't a pilgrim anymore. I was different from the girl who came to Spain, but didn't know who I'd be when I went home after this experience.

I definitely didn't want to go back to how I was. My throat constricted in those four steps to the arch.

I walked up to the pillar, ready to put my hand on it and start bowing. In the Tree of Jesse, sunk in the middle of the carved faces and torsos of various Old Testament men, is a handprint. It is not a flat hand, of the same depth all the way across. The fingers are deeper, and so your hand sinks right in the pillar, as if you were clutching the Tree of Jesse. My fingers sunk in much deeper than I even thought they would when I saw the handprint, more than an inch deep into the marble. I gasped and grasped at it, holding tight to the marble, clenching it in my hand. My hand fit perfectly, as though it was always meant to be there.

The handprint was not carved by the artist. It was created by millions of hands clutching that pillar as they enter the cathedral, ending their pilgrimage. I stood there for many seconds with my hand in the Tree of Jesse, amazed. Then I remembered I was supposed to bow three times and stick my hand in the fish's mouth. I did that, and then started to cry and giggle simultaneously.

We walked through the cathedral and got on another line. It led us under the altar where the remains of James sat in a silver chest behind a glass wall. I knelt down and tried to say a prayer, thanking Saint James for his prayers in getting me there, as the stern guard instructed me to do, but I couldn't concentrate. There was not a thought in my head. I was still giggling.

The giggling reached fever pitch when we got on a third line and climbed up steps to the back of the altar, where a large bronze statue of Saint James, his armor studded with colored glass, gazed down on the people in the church with a frozen, bug-eyed stare. When it was my turn, I did just what I saw everyone else before me do and put my arms around the statue, scraping the inside of my arms on his glass decorations (maybe they were all rubies and sapphires—who knows?) and squeezed. And then the giggling turned into flat-out uncontrolled laughter.

After we'd done all the things that seemed to make up the end of the Camino de Santiago, Alex and I wandered back to the huge plaza in front of the cathedral, found our way to the hotel, dumped our bags, and fell asleep. I was no longer a pilgrim.

I WAS GLAD there were rituals at the end of the pilgrimage, otherwise I don't know what I would have done. I probably would have fallen apart. Instead, I got there and had something to do. Would the rituals have been more powerful if I knew why I was doing them? Maybe, or maybe not.

In some rituals I've been part of there has been the sense of time and space somehow becoming sacred through the ritual, a sense that we have somehow tapped into the holy or the divine. Like at the Easter Vigil—I swear it gets me every single year. It's dark in the church, and there has been no music, no decoration for days before that. The only light comes from the candles we hold against the deep darkness as creation story after creation story is read. We are transported back to the very beginning of time. But then . . . there is light. The world has been re-created once more, and the lights in the church are thrown on and it is filled with flowers and the organ and trumpets peal out and we break into song. There is hope for a new life, a new creation. I cry every time. But in the rituals at the end of the Camino, there was none of that. It felt more as though one had better do something physical, something tangible, or fall apart.

When my mother, sister, and I got to the hospital, after my

father died, the first thing my mother thought to do when she got up to the floor and saw the nurses waiting for her outside his room was to call the Catholic priest and ask him to come anoint my father.

"Oh, Mrs. Egan," he said, "anointing is for the living. I anointed him last week. I'm eating my dinner now."

"Oh, okay," my mother said. "Sorry to bother you."

He did not come up.

My mother didn't really want the anointing of the sick. She didn't know what she wanted, she just knew she had to do something. And she was right. She did need that. We all need that when reality is simply too big.

Ritual can transform space and time, can help us tap into the holy. But I think sometimes we just need it to have something small to do because we cannot comprehend the big right then. We need small pieces to hold on to.

31.

> *Prayer [is] . . . the reflexion immediately preceding the act of letting oneself fall.*
>
> —KARL RAHNER

At the pilgrims' Mass the day after we arrived in Santiago, hundreds of people packed the cathedral as tightly as possible, spilling out through the doors and into the wide plazas. Dozens of youth groups sang and shouted chants while others waved huge banners and flags. Pilgrims who had walked hundreds of miles to reach this place, backpacks and dust still clinging to them, cried. People dressed up as Saint James himself, in brown burlap robes, rope sandals, and floppy hats milled around. A drum corps, sixty people strong, wearing white robes with long red crosses on the front boomed their way through the center aisle to the front of the nave.

At the end of Mass, there was a pause and hush as six burly Franciscans appeared and slowly unraveled a thick rope wound around a pillar in front of the altar.

"They are going to swing the *botafumeiro*!" I heard whispered and then shouted as the largest incense burner I have ever seen slowly descended on the other end of that rope from the rafters high above the crossing.

Shaped just like the small incense burner used in your local parish church, the brass *botafumeiro* was almost as tall as the priest as it hung shining just a few inches off the ground. Holding a fistful of burning incense sticks, the priest opened the little door on the side of the *botafumeiro,* shoved the already thickly smoking incense inside, slammed the door shut, and gave it a gentle push.

The *botafumeiro* swayed about six inches in either direction across the front of the altar at first, but when it reached the low point of its arc, the six monks gave the rope a jerk. The *botafumeiro* swung out another foot or so. The monks kept tugging the rope, ever increasing the height the *botafumeiro* swung. Soft clouds of scented smoke poured out of the censer.

The *botafumeiro* climbed all the way up till it was swinging over the entire congregation, to the farthest reaches of the cathedral, a hundred feet out in either direction. It swung so high that it caught with a jolt at the top of its arc and orange flames jumped out from the vents before it swung back down over our heads with an audible roar and groaning of rope. I was not breathing air but rather scent, pure and inescapable scent with every breath. The sunlight pierced through the stained-glass windows, and suddenly the gray billows of smoke were swirling masses of color moving in front of me.

Overwhelmed by smell, surrounded by color, I heard beautiful music—bells, or French horns, or people singing—a piercing noise that shook me as deeply as the smoke filled me. I had never heard anything like it.

The cantor called out "*¡Tranquilo!*" but it was too late. People were shouting and laughing, some were crying, and one person fainted. Though jostled and crammed, too many of us standing in this space, no one argued or pushed. Instead we became one moving, undulating mass, swinging and swaying with the smoke and the colors and the flashing *botafumeiro*. It felt as though my body had turned to laughter, and for just a moment I felt a burning and surging love for all these people surrounding me. I wanted to kiss each one.

When the *botafumeiro* finally ran out of smoke, a large young man positioned himself on the altar, ready to tackle. As the *botafumeiro* swung past him, he lunged forward, grabbed the giant chains, and violently spun around, fizzling out the momentum. The church could take it no more, bursting into frenzied applause. The youth groups started singing again.

The cantor yelled, *"¡Tranquilo! Tranquilo!"*

We walked out of the cathedral into the sun. "That was the most amazing thing I have ever seen," I said. Alex nodded. "The smell and the colors and the music—"

"What music?" he asked.

"The music they played while they swung that thing."

"There was no music. Don't you remember the guy yelling at us to be silent?"

I did remember that and now I was confused.

"No one was playing or singing, Kerry."

Whether or not anyone played or sang in that church, I did hear music, the sweetest and clearest sound I have ever heard.

Afterword

I live in Iowa now with my husband, Alex, and our two chocolate Labrador retrievers. Our house is in an old neighborhood called Goosetown, named after the geese that the original Bohemian settlers once allowed to patrol up and down the brick streets. Like Galicia, everything grows exuberantly in Iowa, although I am now surrounded by cornfields instead of wheat. There's an eighty-year-old peony hedge in front of our house; apple, cherry, and pear trees in the side yard; and a long narrow backyard where women once grew hundred-foot lines of vegetables for their families.

When I first got home from the pilgrimage a few years ago, I worried that I would never be able to pick up where I'd left off, because I felt so different. But in fact, I fell seamlessly back into the routines and responsibilities of my life. That sense of wonder and amazement that developed in Santiago remained and colored everything I did for a little while; for a few months I walked around feeling like everything glowed. But then, slowly, and without my even noticing it, the feeling faded away.

Most modern accounts of pilgrimage on the Camino end in the cathedral. The writers don't say what happens when they go home, as though the story stopped when they were doused by the *botafumeiro.* While critics often question or complain about this, I think there's an excellent reason for it: If you go on pilgrimage, life won't be radically transformed when you get back. The same responsibilities are there, and the same problems are waiting. Going on pilgrimage doesn't change that.

Maybe this isn't the case with everyone. Maybe that woman from Barcelona had twelve fantastic job offers within weeks of returning home, maybe that couple overcame their infertility, maybe that guy looking for a wife met a beautiful, smart, funny woman in Santiago and they eloped that night. But when I returned to Massachusetts, I still had to face my past, and my loss. The Camino didn't take it away just because I returned feeling all magical and blessed. I grieved long and hard, and it sometimes felt like my insides were coming out. But I did it differently than I would have otherwise, and perhaps this was really the Camino's gift. Life didn't change, but perspective did.

Many times on the Camino the road seemed to stretch out over the wide open hills to pass through a town or cross a stream. But inevitably, what clearly seemed to be the Camino was in fact not, and the road twisted away in a completely unexpected direction. Sometimes this led to disappointment, or an unexpected shady spot, but usually it led to general confusion and disorientation. This experience of learning to not count on what I thought would happen, while it may seem a bit obvious now, had a profound effect on me when I got back. I had learned that I really didn't need to know too much more than the next two steps I needed to take, because if I did I would be convinced I couldn't make it all the way to Santiago. And so I learned I didn't need to worry about how I would rethink my entire worldview on a single Thursday afternoon. This made the roller coaster of grief bearable.

By the end of the pilgrimage, it became easy to rest in the safety of the Camino—the purpose and pattern of one's days, the generosity of the people along the way, the steadiness of the road itself, the unexpected and unexplainable presence of God. It's harder to be aware of God now, harder to trust, harder to allow myself to fall. I can go for weeks on end without thinking about or noticing God in the course of my day. On the Camino, that was impossible. The churches, standing crosses, and other outward signs of Christianity that reminded one of God were all over. But more important were the days with nothing to do but walk and breathe and listen. Listening is the hard part now.

AT THE BACK of our yard in Iowa is a white barn. It's big enough for only one horse or maybe two mules. The people who built it a hundred years ago wouldn't have had more than that to put in there. Our car doesn't fit, so it houses the lawn mower and some shovels. Grass grows on the roof and light breaks in through the cracks between the warped boards, once whitewashed, now dirty. There is a giant hole four feet wide and two feet deep in the dirt floor. Wasps live in the rafters.

There is something that feels undeniably sacred when standing in that barn. I'm not the only one who feels it. Everyone whispers in there. And it isn't just this barn. Most barns in the Midwest have the same effect on people, from the smallest to the most elaborate three-story circular barns. Something in the air feels grand and still and holy.

I've heard that when European immigrants moved to the

American prairie the only big structures people knew how to build were churches; consequently, barns are built on the same proportions as cathedrals and chapels. If this is true, then maybe barns feel sacred to me because I've been conditioned to sense God in buildings of specific proportions. Maybe the barn is a spiritual mnemonic device, the sort of thing that was all over the place on the Camino, but missing now. Maybe it isn't that the sacred is somehow more present on the Camino or that God lives in northern Spain. Perhaps it is that the Camino makes it easier to sense a God who is always there, but is easy to ignore. A God one has to have courage to fall into, whether through walking or love or grief or, through the final prayer of this pilgrimage, remembering.

Acknowledgments

Just as I would never have been able to walk the Camino de Santiago without the help of many kind and generous people, so I would never have been able to write this book without the support, encouragement, and suggestions of so many. My deepest thanks to everyone who helped me complete this part of the pilgrimage.

Trace Murphy has been an especially kind and patient editor, and Eric Major believed in this book when I didn't quite believe in it myself. My agent Marly Rusoff has been an advocate, cheerleader, and friend through the whole process.

Many people have read the manuscript or parts of it at various stages and have shared their ideas, suggestions, questions, and criticisms. The Rev. Dudley Rose and my Senior Seminar group at Harvard Divinity School helped me think about what this project could be when it was still just an essay. My Clinical Pastoral Education group at New York Methodist Hospital pushed me to think about my relationships with God, family, myself, and the idea of writing a book as only a supportive and compassionate CPE group could do. Katie Ford, Kristin Kaulbach Miles, Amani Brown, and Katie Ives offered observations and insights and asked hard questions.

Sister Jeannette Normandin and Dr. Tziporah Cohen helped me learn how to talk and write about grief, anger, love, and God. I hope they understand just what they have given me and how thankful I am.

My father, James Egan, Jr., never stopped encouraging me till he died and I think he's somehow still rooting for me. My mother, Mary Egan, has given me so much, in so many ways, and at so many times, that it is hard to put my gratitude and love into words. All I can say is thank you. My brothers Dan and Jimmy and my sister Kristine are the best friends I have and tell me to cut the crap out, when need be.

Alex Ruskell makes me laugh harder than any other human being. He has been with me every step of this trip, from the taxi to the airport in Boston, to the FedEx box in Iowa City to mail off the final manuscript. This book would not exist without him, and it is my way of saying, "I love you."